UNLOCK YOUR POTENTIAL: OVERCOME BIAS, UPLIFT YOUR CAREER, TRANSFORM YOUR LIFE

BREAK BARRIERS
BUILD BRILLIANCE
BOLDLY BREAKTHROUGH

DR. STEPHANIE WILSON-COLEMAN

Copyright

Unlock Your Potential: Overcome Bias, Uplift Your Career, Transform Your Life

Copyright © 2024 Stephanie E. Wilson-Coleman,

The Champagne Connection, Chicago IL 60680

www.champagneconnection.com

www.asipofinspiration.com

Cover design by Sadia A

Copyright © 2025 by Dr. Stephanie Wilson-Coleman

All rights reserved. No part of this book may be reproduced, distributed, or transmitted in any form or by any means, including photocopying, recording, or other electronic or mechanical methods, without the prior written permission of the publisher, except in the case of brief quotations embodied in critical reviews and certain other noncommercial uses permitted by copyright law.

Published by The Champagne Connection, Inc. P O BOX 87468, Chicago, IL 60680

ISBN: 979-8-9922061-0-4 First Edition: 2025

Cover design by Sadia A

Interior design by Sadia A

Printed in the United States of America

For permissions, inquiries, or to request additional copies, contact:

sewc@champagneconnection.com

The content within this book is based on the author's personal experiences, research, and insights. While every effort has been made to ensure accuracy, the author and publisher assume no responsibility for errors or omissions or for any consequences resulting from the use of the information herein.

Information and/or practices provided in this book are made available with the understanding that the author nor the publisher do not dispense medical advice, nor prescribe the use of any technique as a form of treatment for physical or mental problems without the advice of a physician or health care professional either directly or indirectly.

Library of Congress Control Number: [2025] [Stephanie E Wilson-Coleman]

DEDICATION

This book is dedicated to all minority women striving to overcome obstacles and achieve greatness. You are strong, resilient, and capable of anything you set your mind to. May this book be a source of inspiration, guidance, and empowerment as you pursue your goals and aspirations.

Let's begin the journey of Breaking Barriers, Building Brilliance, and Boldly Breaking Through.

PREFACE

As an experienced business leader, I've observed the unique challenges minority women encounter in the workplace. Overcoming these obstacles requires more than grit and determination—it calls for a clear understanding of the environment, a practical set of strategies, and an unwavering belief in oneself. This book is my effort to bridge that gap.

Within these pages, you'll find a guide to navigating the complexities of professional and personal life. I believe empowerment begins with knowledge and self-awareness. Through relatable examples and actionable steps, my goal is to provide you with the tools to advocate for your needs, build resilience, and confidently pursue the success you deserve.

Table of Contents

INTRODUCTION ix

CHAPTER 1----UNDERSTANDING YOUR ENVIRONMENT
    RECOGNIZING WORKPLACE DYNAMICS 1
    IDENTIFYING MICROAGGRESSIONS 4
    NAVIGATING TOKENISM 10
    BUILDING RESILIENCE 16
    ASSESSING PERSONAL BOUNDARIES 21

CHAPTER 2----LEADERSHIP DEVELOPMENT
    DEFINING YOUR LEADERSHIP STYLE 29
    MASTERING COMMUNICATION SKILLS 34
    BUILDING CONFIDENCE AS A LEADER 42
    MENTORSHIP AND SPONSORSHIP 49
    LEADING WITH EMPATHY 56

CHAPTER 3----FINANCIAL EMPOWERMENT
    UNDERSTANDING FINANCIAL LITERACY 61
    BUDGETING FOR SUCCESS 67
    OVERCOMING FINANCIAL BARRIERS 78
    CREATING MULTIPLE INCOME STREAMS 83

CHAPTER 4----BUILDING MEANINGFUL ALLIANCES
    NETWORKING WITH PURPOSE 89
    COLLABORATION OVER COMPETITION 94
    ALLYSHIP AND ADVOCACY 99
    LEVERAGING SOCIAL CAPITAL 104

CHAPTER 5 -----BALANCING PERSONAL AND PROFESSIONAL LIFE

- TIME MANAGEMENT TECHNIQUES 118
- SETTING PRIORITIES AND GOALS 123
- SELF-CARE AND WELLBEING 128
- MANAGING STRESS AND BURNOUT 134
- CREATING A SUPPORT SYSTEM 139

CHAPTER 6 -----ADVOCATING FOR YOURSELF 146

- ARTICULATING YOUR VALUE 146
- NEGOTIATING FOR WHAT YOU DESERVE 150
- CONFRONTING BIAS AND DISCRIMINATION 154
- CELEBRATING SUCCESS AND GROWTH 166

ACKNOWLEDGMENTS 173

APPENDIX 174

- LIST OF SEVERAL ORGANIZATIONS SUPPORTING MINORITY WOMEN 174
- RECOMMENDED READING 175
- PERSONAL DEVELOPMENT & SELF-EMPOWERMENT 176
- LEADERSHIP & CAREER ADVANCEMENT 176
- ENTREPRENEURSHIP & FINANCIAL SUCCESS 177
- RESILIENCE & MENTAL WELLNESS 178
- INSPIRATIONAL STORIES 178
- FINANCIAL LITERACY RESOURCES 179
- ORGANIZATIONS AND PROGRAMS 179
- WORKSHOPS AND COACHING 181

ADVISORS AND NETWORKS 181
BOOKS AND ONLINE COURSES 182
GLOSSARY 184

INTRODUCTION

In today's world, hard work alone isn't enough to guarantee success. For minority women, the playing field is often uneven. We frequently encounter systemic biases, unconscious prejudices, and the weight of societal expectations that can hinder our opportunities.

This book isn't about dwelling on the challenges; it's about equipping you with the skills and strategies to rise above them. It's about embracing the unique strength and brilliance you bring to every room, every conversation, and every opportunity.

This book serves as your guide to navigating the intricacies of your professional and personal life, empowering you to:

Recognize and address workplace dynamics: Recognize microaggressions, grasp the concept of tokenism, and develop resilience to effectively navigate challenging situations.

Develop strong leadership skills: Identify your leadership style, enhance your communication skills, and cultivate the confidence to lead with empathy and impact.

Achieve financial empowerment: Gain a solid understanding of financial literacy, design realistic budgets, explore investment opportunities, and break through economic barriers.

Build meaningful alliances: Develop strategic networking skills, create collaborative environments, and utilize your social connections to drive growth.

Balance personal and professional life: Adopt practical time management strategies, align your actions with your goals, and commit to self-care to enhance your overall well-being.

Advocate for yourself: Clearly articulate your value, negotiate confidently for what you deserve, address bias head-on, and advocate for inclusivity and diversity.

This journey extends beyond your career—it's about creating a life filled with purpose, fulfillment, and meaningful impact.

Are you ready to step into your strength and achieve your success? Let's get started.

CHAPTER 1

UNDERSTANDING YOUR ENVIRONMENT

RECOGNIZING WORKPLACE DYNAMICS

The professional world, especially for minority women, is filled with both opportunities and challenges. Understanding the unique dynamics at play in the workplace is essential for navigating it successfully. This is where self-awareness, combined with strategic thinking, becomes your guiding tool.

Picture this: You walk into a meeting and immediately notice that you're the only woman of color in the room. A subtle shift in the room's energy may leave you feeling uneasy. For many minority women, this is a familiar experience—a constant awareness of being observed, of standing out as "the other" in spaces that often seem unwelcoming.

One prominent workplace challenge is the **"glass ceiling"** effect—an invisible barrier that prevents women, especially minority women, from advancing into senior leadership roles. The factors behind this are multifaceted, including ingrained biases, limited access to sponsorship and mentorship, and the ongoing challenge of balancing career growth with family responsibilities.

Another critical issue to recognize is **tokenism**—the practice of hiring or promoting a small number of minority individuals to create a superficial appearance of inclusivity. While this may seem progressive at first glance, it often results in feelings of isolation and heightened pressure. As a token minority employee, you might feel excessively scrutinized or burdened with representing an entire group.

Microaggressions present yet another persistent challenge for minority women. These subtle and often unintentional actions or remarks can have profound effects, fostering feelings of marginalization and invalidation. Examples include being asked to explain your cultural background or being told that you "speak well" for a person of color. Though seemingly minor, such comments can erode confidence and a sense of belonging over time.

These challenges are just a few of the dynamics shaping the workplace experience for minority women. While they may seem overwhelming, understanding these dynamics is a crucial first step in addressing them effectively. Consider the following questions to help you recognize these patterns in your own workplace:

Do you feel like your voice is truly heard and valued? If your contributions are often overlooked or dismissed, it may indicate a lack of inclusivity or an environment that does not support diverse perspectives.

Do you notice many women, particularly women of color, in leadership positions? If not, this could suggest the presence of a glass ceiling or a lack of diversity within the organization.

Are there specific incidents or comments that make you feel uncomfortable or disrespected? These could be examples of microaggressions. Pay attention to these experiences and consider strategies to address them constructively.

Do you feel pressure to represent your entire community or group? This is a hallmark of tokenism. Remember, you are an individual with unique skills and experiences—not a representative of an entire demographic.

Recognizing these workplace dynamics isn't about focusing solely on the challenges but about empowering yourself to take charge. Awareness of these issues allows you to address them proactively, build resilience, and advocate effectively for yourself.

The next chapter will provide actionable strategies for identifying and responding to microaggressions, a persistent issue in many workplaces. By learning to recognize and confront these subtle biases, you can contribute to creating a more equitable and inclusive environment for yourself and others.

IDENTIFYING MICROAGGRESSIONS

Imagine a busy office environment filled with the hum of conversations, the clatter of keyboards, and the occasional burst of laughter. It's a scene familiar to many, yet for minority women, navigating this space can feel like walking through a maze of subtle biases and unspoken expectations. These biases, often disguised as harmless interactions, can erode confidence and stall career progress. These moments are known as microaggressions, and understanding them is the first step toward addressing their impact.

Microaggressions are subtle, often unintentional, yet deeply ingrained forms of discrimination. They feel like tiny pinpricks that, over time, can leave you constantly on guard, belittled, or misunderstood. They take many forms, such as questioning your expertise or attributing your success to affirmative action rather than your merit.

Here are some common examples of microaggressions that minority women face in the workplace.

"You speak English so well." Although intended as a compliment, this statement subtly implies that the recipient's proficiency in English is surprising. It reinforces the stereotype that minorities are not fluent in the dominant language and can leave the individual feeling as though their identity as a proficient speaker is not fully acknowledged.

"Where are you really from?" This question is often posed to minority women, even when they clearly identify with their nationality. It can feel intrusive and suggest a lack of acceptance of their claimed identity, casting doubt on their belonging.

"You're so articulate." While seemingly positive, this comment reinforces the stereotype that minority women are not expected to be articulate. It can feel as though you're being praised for something that should be considered standard, underscoring unspoken assumptions about your communication abilities.

"You're so aggressive." This remark, often directed at women of color who assert their opinions or disagree with colleagues, perpetuates the harmful stereotype that women of color are inherently aggressive. It marginalizes assertive expression and can create a sense of being penalized for speaking up.

"You're so pretty for a Black woman." While appearing complimentary, this statement perpetuates the damaging idea that beauty standards are different for women of color. It can feel objectifying and diminishes one's value by reducing it to physical appearance.

These microaggressions are often difficult to address directly because they occur in seemingly casual or well-meaning conversations. The person making the comment may not even recognize the harm caused by their words. However, their impact can be profound, leading to feelings of isolation, frustration, and the exhausting need to constantly prove oneself.

STRATEGIES FOR RESPONDING TO MICROAGGRESSIONS

So, how can you navigate these encounters effectively? Here are some strategies to help you respond to microaggressions with both grace and assertiveness:

Pause and Reflect: Before reacting impulsively, take a moment to process what you've heard. Does the comment come from a place of genuine ignorance, or does it carry an underlying bias?

Reframe the Comment: Challenge implicit bias by reframing the comment to address the subtle message. For example, if someone says, "You speak English so well," you could respond, "Thank you! Communication has always been important to me, and I've worked hard to refine my skills."

Educate and Explain: If you feel comfortable, gently educate the person about the impact of their words. For example, you might say, "I know you meant that as a compliment, but comments like that can reinforce stereotypes."

Assert Yourself: Don't hesitate to address overtly offensive comments directly. You can say, "That remark is inappropriate," or "I find that comment disrespectful." Assertiveness can set clear boundaries while reinforcing your self-respect.

Seek Support: Build a supportive network of friends, family, or colleagues to confide in. Sharing your experiences can help you process your feelings and gain valuable perspectives from others who understand. Remember, you're not alone in facing these challenges.

Document the Incident: If the microaggressions are recurring or severe, document the incidents in detail. This record can be invaluable if you need to report the issue to HR or other authorities.

Focus on Your Strengths: Always remember that microaggressions do not define your value or abilities. Concentrate on your strengths, accomplishments, and the positive aspects of your work to maintain confidence.

Self-Care: Prioritize your well-being by engaging in activities that bring you joy and relaxation. Taking care of yourself is essential, especially when navigating challenging situations.

Beyond the Workplace: Microaggressions can occur in various areas of life, from social settings to family interactions. Staying aware of these biases in all contexts can help you address them more effectively.

The Power of Collective Action: You're not alone in addressing these challenges. Sharing your experiences, educating others, and advocating for change contribute to dismantling the systems that perpetuate microaggressions. Collective efforts can lead to greater awareness, understanding, and inclusion across all areas of life.

Building Resilience: Recognizing microaggressions is the first step in building resilience. Equip yourself with tools to navigate these situations without compromising your self-esteem or career goals. By identifying, responding to, and ultimately addressing microaggressions, you empower yourself to create a more inclusive environment for everyone.

A PERSONAL STORY:

I'll never forget the time I was in a business meeting presenting a new marketing strategy. My ideas were met with enthusiasm, but when I suggested a bold move, a senior colleague chuckled and said, "Well, that's very ambitious for someone so young." Although delivered with a seemingly harmless tone, the comment left me feeling deflated and questioning my abilities. My age was used to diminish my expertise and contributions—a classic example of a microaggression.

That experience strengthened my resolve to confront these biases. I became more mindful of subtle prejudices and developed strategies to respond effectively. I also began educating others about the impact of these comments and found allies within my company who supported me in fostering a more inclusive culture. It wasn't perfect, but my efforts made a difference.

MOVING FORWARD:

Microaggressions are a complex issue that requires awareness and proactive action. By recognizing these subtle forms of bias, understanding their impact, and developing effective strategies to address them, we can dismantle the systems that perpetuate them. This is a journey of empowerment, self-awareness, and collective action.

Together, we can create a world where minority women thrive, confident and empowered in every aspect of their lives.

NAVIGATING TOKENISM

Have you ever felt like the only one in the room who looked like you? Or perhaps you've been acknowledged for your "diversity" rather than your skills and accomplishments? These experiences often signify tokenism—a subtle yet harmful form of discrimination that can leave minority women feeling isolated, undervalued, and underutilized.

Tokenism can appear in many forms: being the only woman of color in a meeting, repeatedly asked to speak on behalf of an entire community, or receiving recognition for simply being present. While these scenarios may seem harmless on the surface, they often stem from unconscious biases and a lack of genuine commitment to inclusion. The true harm of tokenism lies in its ability to create the illusion of progress while reinforcing existing power imbalances.

So, how can you navigate the challenges of tokenism and ensure your voice is heard, your talents are recognized, and your individuality is celebrated? Here are some strategies to help you reclaim your confidence and excel in your professional journey:

1. **Understand the Dynamics:** Recognize that tokenism is a real issue and not a product of your imagination. Reflect on your experiences and pinpoint situations where you felt like a token representative. Pay attention to the language used, the roles you're assigned, and the expectations placed upon you. Understanding these dynamics will prepare you to respond more effectively.

2. **Challenge Assumptions:** Don't shy away from challenging stereotypes and biases. If you're often asked to speak about your culture or background, politely but firmly redirect the conversation to your expertise and contributions. For example, instead of answering, "Can you tell us about your experience being a woman of color in this industry?" you might say, "I'm happy to share my perspective on how diversity can drive our team's success."

3. **Focus on Your Strengths:** Don't let tokenism overshadow your identity. Emphasize your strengths, skills, and accomplishments. Showcase your expertise and prove your value through measurable results. Build a robust professional portfolio that highlights your achievements and contributions.

4. **Find Your Allies:** Cultivate a network of allies who can provide support and guidance. Seek mentors and sponsors who understand the challenges of being a minority woman and are invested in your success. Connect with peers in your field who share similar experiences to form a supportive community.

5. **Speak Up and Advocate:** When faced with tokenism or any form of bias, use your voice to address it. Challenge discriminatory practices and advocate for change. Take the initiative to promote inclusivity and diversity within your organization.

6. **Embrace Your Individuality:** Tokenism often reduces people to stereotypes, erasing their individuality. Celebrate your unique experiences, talents, and perspectives. Express yourself authentically and let your true self shine.

7. **Practice Self-Care:** Navigating tokenism can be emotionally taxing. Prioritize self-care to nurture your

mental and emotional well-being. Engage in activities that bring you joy, lean on supportive friends and family, and set boundaries to protect your energy and time.

8. **Don't Accept the Status Quo:** Reject the notion of being a token. Strive to be recognized as a valuable and respected team member. Seek opportunities to grow, learn, and advance in your career.

9. **Seek Opportunities for Mentorship:** Mentorship can be instrumental in navigating workplace challenges. Find experienced professionals who can offer guidance and share their insights. Use their advice to overcome obstacles and achieve your goals.

10. **Be a Role Model:** As you navigate tokenism, remember that your resilience and determination can inspire others. By embracing your individuality and advocating for change, you can help create a more equitable and inclusive work environment for everyone.

REAL-LIFE STORIES:

Let's explore real-life examples that illustrate the challenges of tokenism and the strategies used to navigate them. The names have been changed to ensure anonymity.

Anya, a skilled software engineer, was often the only woman of color in her team meetings. She noticed a troubling pattern: her male colleagues frequently asked her to provide "the minority perspective," even on topics unrelated to diversity or inclusion. Recognizing the need to address this, Anya responded politely but firmly: "I appreciate your interest in my perspective, but I'm here to contribute my technical expertise and problem-solving skills." She then redirected the discussion to the technical details at hand. By calmly steering the conversation, Anya reinforced her authority and emphasized her core contributions. She also made it clear that she was not a spokesperson for her entire race or gender.

Maya, a marketing manager, was repeatedly praised for her "cultural sensitivity" instead of her groundbreaking marketing campaigns. While she appreciated the acknowledgment of her cultural understanding, it felt like her true abilities were being overshadowed. Maya recognized the need to change the narrative. She began highlighting her strategic thinking, analytical skills, and results-driven approach during team meetings and presentations. Additionally, she sought out opportunities to mentor junior colleagues, demonstrating her leadership capabilities. By showcasing her expertise and taking on leadership roles, Maya successfully shifted the focus from her cultural background to her professional achievements.

Sarah, a financial analyst, found herself frequently overlooked for promotions despite consistently exceeding expectations. She realized that her reluctance to self-promote and lack of visibility were barriers to her career growth. Determined to change this, Sarah started attending industry events and conferences to network with senior leaders. She also took the initiative to lead projects that expanded her skills and increased her visibility. Her efforts paid off: Sarah earned a promotion and gained the recognition she deserved. Her story highlights the importance of taking initiative, seeking opportunities, and building meaningful relationships to achieve your goals.

Tokenism is a nuanced and often subtle issue. It can be insidious and, at times, unintentional. However, by recognizing the underlying dynamics, challenging biases, embracing your individuality, and advocating for meaningful change, you can equip yourself to navigate tokenism and succeed in your professional journey.

Remember, you are not alone. Many minority women have faced similar challenges and emerged stronger. By sharing your experiences, supporting one another, and advocating for a more inclusive workplace, we can collectively contribute to creating a fairer and more equitable world for everyone.

BUILDING RESILIENCE

The professional journey of a minority woman can be filled with unique challenges. In this path, resilience is not merely an asset—it is a necessity. Building resilience isn't about becoming immune to difficulties; it's about cultivating the strength to face them with grace, determination, and an unwavering sense of self-worth. It's about understanding that setbacks aren't failures but opportunities to learn, adapt, and grow stronger.

Imagine a young woman, Sharon, who recently began her career in a male-dominated field. Despite her brilliance and passion, she faces constant microaggressions and subtle biases. From being overlooked in meetings to having her qualifications questioned, Sharon starts to doubt her abilities and loses her initial confidence. But she remains determined to succeed. Sharon realizes that resilience doesn't mean ignoring or suppressing these experiences—it means confronting them head-on.

Sharon begins by educating herself about unconscious bias. She learns how stereotypes and implicit assumptions influence perceptions, even in seemingly neutral situations. This knowledge empowers her to reframe those microaggressions, recognizing them not as personal attacks but as reflections of others' unconscious biases.

Next, Sharon builds a support system. She seeks out mentors and sponsors who provide guidance and encouragement. She connects with other women in her field, forming a network of peers who share similar experiences and offer empathy and advice. This network becomes a safe space for Sharon to process her feelings, share challenges, and celebrate successes.

Sharon also prioritizes self-care, understanding its critical role in maintaining her mental and emotional well-being. She makes time for activities that bring her joy, such as walking in nature, reading a book, or spending time with loved ones. She establishes boundaries, recognizing that she is not obligated to endure every microaggression or tolerate disrespectful behavior.

Building resilience isn't a quick fix—it's a continuous journey of self-discovery and growth. It involves acknowledging your emotions, understanding your strengths and weaknesses, and developing strategies to cope with stress and adversity. Resilience means learning to bounce back from setbacks—not just physically, but emotionally and mentally as well.

HERE ARE SOME PRACTICAL STRATEGIES TO CULTIVATE RESILIENCE:

1. Embrace Mindfulness and Self-Awareness:

- Practice mindfulness meditation: This practice helps you stay present in the moment, recognizing your thoughts and emotions without judgment. It can provide clarity and emotional stability during challenging situations.
- Journal your experiences: Regularly writing about your experiences, both positive and negative, can help you process emotions, identify patterns, and gain insights into your thought processes.
- Engage in self-reflection: Take time to reflect on your experiences, analyzing your responses to challenges. This practice helps you understand your triggers, develop coping strategies, and deepen self-awareness.

2. Develop Healthy Coping Mechanisms:

- Exercise regularly: Physical activity releases endorphins that boost your mood, alleviate stress, and improve sleep quality, all contributing to mental and emotional resilience.
- Seek support from trusted individuals: Sharing your experiences with a therapist, counselor, close

friend, or family member can provide a safe space to process emotions and gain valuable insights.
- Engage in activities you enjoy: Dedicate time to hobbies and activities that bring you joy and relaxation. These serve as outlets for stress and help maintain a positive outlook.

3. Learn to Reframe Challenges:
- Focus on the positive: Instead of dwelling on negative experiences, identify lessons learned and growth opportunities within challenging situations.
- Practice gratitude: Expressing gratitude for even small blessings can shift your mindset and help you focus on the positive aspects of your life.
- Develop a growth mindset: View challenges as opportunities for learning and growth rather than as threats or failures.

4. Build a Supportive Network:
- Cultivate meaningful connections: Surround yourself with people who uplift you and support your personal and professional growth.
- Join professional organizations or support groups: These spaces can provide valuable connections with like-minded individuals, platforms for sharing experiences, and access to resources and support.

- Seek out mentors and sponsors: Mentors and sponsors can offer guidance, support, and advocacy, helping you navigate challenges and achieve your goals.

5. Practice Self-Compassion:

- Recognize that everyone makes mistakes: Be kind to yourself when setbacks occur. Learn from mistakes and move forward with compassion.
- Celebrate your successes: Take time to acknowledge and appreciate your accomplishments, no matter how small they may seem.
- Focus on self-care: Prioritize your physical, mental, and emotional well-being.

Resilience isn't about being unaffected by challenges; it's about learning to navigate them effectively. By developing mental and emotional strength, adopting healthy coping mechanisms, and building a supportive network, you can thrive in any environment. Embrace life's inevitable bumps as opportunities for growth and self-discovery.

Remember, Sharon's journey is just one example. Countless other minority women have faced similar challenges and emerged stronger, more resilient, and more determined to achieve their goals. Their experiences offer invaluable lessons, reminding us that resilience is not a destination but a journey of continuous growth. By adopting these strategies, you can build the resilience to overcome obstacles, seize opportunities, and achieve your goals.

ASSESSING PERSONAL BOUNDARIES

The ability to set and maintain personal boundaries is essential for achieving a healthy work-life balance. It's about recognizing your limitations, valuing your time and energy, and ensuring that professional responsibilities don't overshadow your personal well-being. This is especially important for minority women, who often navigate demanding professional environments while managing societal pressures and expectations.

Imagine Sarah, a skilled marketing manager who consistently exceeds expectations at work. She frequently takes on additional projects and works late into the night to meet deadlines. However, this unwavering dedication comes at a significant cost. Sarah feels constantly stressed, neglects her personal life, and is on the brink of burnout. Her story is far from unique—it underscores the importance of setting personal boundaries to protect mental and emotional health and prevent burnout.

How can you identify and establish these boundaries? It's a process of self-reflection and effective communication. It requires understanding your values, recognizing your limits, and confidently asserting your needs to others.

1. **Understanding Your Values:** The first step in establishing boundaries is understanding your core values. What matters most to you? Is it spending quality time with family, pursuing personal passions, or having the space to relax and recharge? Once you identify your values, you can use them as a guide to make decisions and prioritize activities that align with your goals.

   For instance, if spending time with family is a priority, you might set a boundary to avoid working on weekends, ensuring you have dedicated time for family gatherings or activities.

2. **Recognizing Your Limits:** Everyone has limits—both physical and emotional. It's important to be aware of your own boundaries and recognize when you're nearing your capacity. This could mean being mindful of your workload, identifying when you're feeling overwhelmed, or acknowledging when it's time to step back from a task.

A helpful strategy is to identify your triggers—situations or behaviors that often leave you feeling stressed or drained. Once you understand these triggers, you can create strategies to manage them. For example, if long meetings tend to exhaust you, you might set a timer for yourself or schedule breaks to avoid prolonged fatigue.

3.Communicating Your Boundaries: Once you've identified your values and limits, the next step is to communicate them to others. This can feel challenging at first, especially for minority women who may have been conditioned to prioritize agreeability and avoid confrontation.

However, assertively expressing your needs is crucial for achieving a sustainable work-life balance. Clear communication helps others understand your boundaries and ensures that your time and energy are respected.

HERE ARE A FEW TIPS FOR COMMUNICATING YOUR BOUNDARIES:

1. **Be Clear and Concise:** When expressing your boundaries, be direct and specific. Avoid vague language that could lead to misunderstandings. For example, instead of saying, "I'm too busy," try, "I'm already committed to several projects and won't be able to take on anything new at this time."

2. **Use "I" Statements:** Focus on your own needs and feelings by using "I" statements, which help avoid placing blame on others. For instance, instead of saying, "You're always asking me to do extra work," you might say, "I feel overwhelmed when I'm asked to take on additional tasks beyond my current workload."

3. **Practice Empathy:** While communicating your boundaries, it's important to be empathetic and understanding. Acknowledge the other person's perspective while maintaining your limits. For example, you could say, "I understand you're in a challenging situation, and I'm happy to help where I can, but I'm not able to take on this additional task right now."

4. **Be Prepared to Say "No":** Saying "no" is a crucial aspect of setting boundaries. Remember, you don't have to justify or apologize for declining a request that doesn't align with your values or exceeds your limits.

5. **Enforcing Your Boundaries:** Setting boundaries is just the first step; enforcing them is equally important. This means being consistent in your communication and actions, even when it feels uncomfortable. When someone tries to push your boundaries, politely but firmly restate your position.

For instance, if a colleague asks you to work late on a project despite your prior commitment to leaving early, you could say, "I appreciate you asking, but I've already made a commitment to leave at [time] today. I'm happy to discuss it further tomorrow when I'm back in the office."

6. **Handling Pushback:** It's common to face resistance when setting and enforcing boundaries. People may try to guilt-trip you, dismiss your needs, or make you feel obligated to comply with their requests. Remember, you have the right to establish boundaries, and you don't need to justify your decisions to anyone.

- **Don't engage in arguments:** If someone challenges your boundaries, avoid getting defensive or engaging in arguments. Stay calm and reiterate your position clearly and concisely.
- **Don't feel obligated to explain:** You don't have to provide detailed explanations for your boundaries. A simple response like, "I'm not comfortable with that" or "I've already made a decision" is sufficient.
- **Stay firm and consistent:** If someone continues to push back, remain steadfast and consistent in your response. Resist the pressure to give in or feel guilty.

EXAMPLES OF PERSONAL BOUNDARIES IN THE WORKPLACE:

Time Management: Set boundaries around your work hours, such as refusing to work on weekends or holidays. Clearly communicate your availability to ensure your personal time is respected.

Communication: Establish preferences for how you'd like to receive communication (e.g., email instead of phone calls) and set expectations for response times. For instance, you might let colleagues know you'll respond to emails within 24 hours but won't address non-urgent matters after work hours.

Workload: Define clear limits on the number of projects you're willing to take on or the maximum hours you're prepared to work each week. Being upfront about your capacity helps prevent burnout and ensures you can give your best to each task.

Personal Space: Set boundaries around your physical space in the office. For example, let colleagues know when you need uninterrupted time to focus or establish a designated area for your belongings to maintain organization and privacy.

Social Media: Create clear boundaries regarding personal topics on work-related social media platforms. You might also choose to avoid after-hours communications unless they're urgent, ensuring you maintain a healthy separation between work and personal life.

BENEFITS OF SETTING PERSONAL BOUNDARIES:

Setting and enforcing personal boundaries provides numerous benefits:

- **Improved work-life balance:** Establishing clear boundaries helps separate your professional and personal life, leading to greater fulfillment in both areas.

- **Reduced stress and burnout:** Protecting your mental and emotional well-being through boundaries reduces stress and prevents burnout.
- **Increased productivity:** By focusing on your priorities, you can work more effectively and efficiently, ultimately boosting your productivity.
- **Stronger relationships:** Healthy boundaries improve relationships with colleagues, supervisors, family, and friends by encouraging open communication and mutual respect.
- **Empowerment:** Setting boundaries allows you to assert your individuality and advocate for your needs, fostering a sense of empowerment and confidence.

Setting and maintaining personal boundaries is an ongoing process that requires self-awareness, assertiveness, and commitment. While it may present initial challenges, the benefits far outweigh the difficulties. By establishing these boundaries, you can achieve a healthier and more fulfilling work-life balance, enabling you to thrive both professionally and personally.

CHAPTER 2

LEADERSHIP DEVELOPMENT

DEFINING YOUR LEADERSHIP STYLE

Imagine yourself standing at the crossroads of your professional journey, equipped with tools but unsure which direction to take. You've navigated the challenges of the corporate world, facing microaggressions, the subtle sting of tokenism, and the disheartening weight of being underestimated. Yet, amidst these obstacles, you've unearthed an inner strength—a deep desire to lead, inspire, and make a difference. This is where the process of defining your leadership style begins.

Leadership isn't a one-size-fits-all approach. It's shaped by your values, strengths, and experiences. It's about understanding your unique blend of skills, aligning them with your aspirations, and crafting a leadership style that feels authentic to you.

Start by reflecting on your core values—those guiding principles that shape your actions and decisions. What beliefs are non-negotiable for you? Are you driven by a passion for social justice, a commitment to excellence, or a desire to empower others? These values form the foundation of your leadership style, influencing how you interact with others, make decisions, and lead teams.

Next, identify your strengths—the abilities that set you apart. Are you a visionary thinker, a strategic planner, or an effective communicator? Perhaps you excel at collaboration, problem-solving, or motivating others with compassion. These strengths are your greatest assets, equipping you to succeed in leadership roles.

Once you've identified your values and strengths, explore various leadership styles to find the one that aligns most naturally with your personality and goals. Here are a few common leadership styles to consider:

TRANSFORMATIONAL LEADERSHIP:

This style emphasizes inspiration, vision, and empowering others to achieve their best. Transformational leaders excel at creating a shared vision, instilling a sense of purpose, and challenging others to think creatively. Consider figures like Nelson Mandela, Malala Yousafzai, or Tarana Burke, who sparked movements and empowered people to work toward a better world.

Transactional Leadership: This approach focuses on clear expectations, performance-based rewards, and maintaining a structured work environment. Transactional leaders are adept at setting goals, providing feedback, and ensuring tasks are completed efficiently. Picture a skilled project manager who establishes clear deadlines, monitors progress, and acknowledges achievements.

Servant Leadership: This style prioritizes the needs of others, emphasizing empowerment and support to help team members thrive. Servant leaders are known for humility, empathy, and their focus on building strong relationships. Think of a mentor who offers guidance, encouragement, and a safe environment for personal and professional growth.

Democratic Leadership: This collaborative style encourages open communication and team participation in decision-making. Democratic leaders value input and diverse perspectives, fostering ownership and shared responsibility among team members. Imagine a CEO who holds regular town hall meetings to gather employee feedback and innovative ideas.

Autocratic Leadership: This centralized style involves the leader making all decisions and maintaining strong control over the team. Autocratic leadership can be effective in situations requiring swift action or strict adherence to procedures. However, it's important to weigh the potential drawbacks, such as limited communication and reduced team involvement.

Laissez-faire Leadership: This style offers minimal guidance and supervision, allowing team members to work independently. It can be effective with highly skilled and self-motivated teams but may result in a lack of direction and accountability if not managed carefully.

As you explore these leadership styles, remember that you don't have to adopt just one. Effective leaders often blend elements from different styles to create an approach that suits their unique needs and those of their teams.

For example, you might use a transformational style to inspire and empower your team while incorporating transactional elements to set clear expectations and ensure accountability.

The key is to find a leadership style that feels authentic to you—one that aligns with your values, strengths, and aspirations. It's about embracing your individuality and using your unique abilities to make a meaningful impact.

HERE ARE SOME PRACTICAL TIPS TO HELP YOU DEFINE YOUR LEADERSHIP STYLE:

Self-Reflection: Dedicate time for introspection. Journal your thoughts, reflect on past experiences, and consider the leadership qualities you admire in others. Ask yourself questions like:

- What type of leader do I want to be?
- What are my leadership strengths and weaknesses?
- What values are most important to me?

Feedback Gathering: Seek input from colleagues, mentors, and trusted individuals. Ask for their perspectives on your leadership style and suggestions for further growth. Open communication is essential for gaining a clear understanding of your strengths and areas for improvement.

Mentorship and Observation: Identify mentors who exemplify leadership styles you admire. Observe their behavior, listen to their insights, and learn from their experiences. Mentorship offers valuable guidance and support as you refine your leadership approach.

Experimentation: Don't hesitate to try different leadership techniques. Implement strategies aligned with various styles to discover what works best for you and your team. Continuous learning and adaptation are essential for becoming a more effective leader.

Continuous Improvement: Leadership is a lifelong journey. Stay open to learning and growth. Take advantage of opportunities to develop new skills, attend leadership workshops, and read books on leadership principles. The more you invest in your growth, the more confident and impactful you'll become.

Remember, your leadership style is not static—it evolves as you gain new experiences, refine your skills, and navigate different situations. The key is to stay adaptable, learn from your mistakes, and continuously strive to improve.

This is your story. You are a leader with unique perspectives, experiences, and talents to share with the world. Embrace your individuality, cultivate your leadership style, and embark on a journey of impact and inspiration. The world needs your voice, your vision, and your unwavering commitment to making a difference.

MASTERING COMMUNICATION SKILLS

Communication is the lifeblood of leadership. It's how leaders inspire, motivate, and guide others. For minority women, developing strong communication skills is particularly important, as it enables them to overcome biases, advocate for themselves, and build influence. This section provides tools to help you communicate effectively, build strong relationships, and navigate challenging conversations with confidence.

UNDERSTANDING THE POWER OF COMMUNICATION

Imagine a workplace where your voice carries weight, your ideas resonate, and your vision inspires action. This is the power of effective communication. In leadership, communication goes beyond speaking—it's about understanding, listening, and truly connecting. It's about building relationships rooted in mutual respect and trust, encouraging collaboration, and creating a shared vision for success.

For minority women, effective communication holds unique significance for several reasons:

- Overcoming Biases: In many workplaces, minority women face biases and stereotypes that can hinder their progress. Clear, confident, and empathetic communication can challenge these perceptions and assert their value.

- Building Trust: Establishing trust with colleagues, supervisors, and clients is essential for achieving goals. Strong communication skills help build credibility and rapport, fostering stronger alliances and greater influence.

- Navigating Challenging Conversations: From negotiating salaries to addressing microaggressions, minority women often encounter situations that demand both tact and assertiveness. Effective communication equips them with the tools to approach these conversations with confidence and clarity.

DEVELOPING YOUR COMMUNICATION TOOLBOX

Effective communication is a skill that can be developed and refined with consistent practice. Here are key elements to focus on:

Active Listening: The ability to truly listen and understand another person's perspective is essential for building trust and resolving conflicts. Practice active listening by:

- Paying full attention: Eliminate distractions and maintain eye contact.
- Summarizing and clarifying: Repeat key points to confirm understanding.
- Asking open-ended questions: Encourage the speaker to elaborate and share more details.

- Avoiding interruptions: Allow the speaker to finish their thoughts before responding.

CLEAR AND CONCISE COMMUNICATION:

Expressing your thoughts and ideas clearly and concisely is critical for effective communication. To enhance your skills, focus on:

- Using precise language: Choose words carefully to avoid ambiguity.
- Structuring your thoughts: Organize your message in a logical sequence for better comprehension.
- Incorporating visual aids: Use diagrams, charts, or presentations to enhance understanding when appropriate.
- Seeking feedback: Invite clarification or feedback to ensure your message is received as intended.

NONVERBAL COMMUNICATION

Nonverbal cues, such as body language, tone of voice, and facial expressions, are crucial in delivering your message effectively. To improve your nonverbal communication, consider the following:

Maintain open and relaxed body language: Avoid crossing your arms or fidgeting, as these can signal discomfort or defensiveness.

Use a confident and assertive tone: Speak with clarity and self-assurance to convey credibility.

Smile and make eye contact: These actions reflect warmth and genuine interest, helping build rapport.

Be aware of cultural differences: Recognize and respect variations in body language and nonverbal communication across cultures.

EXAMPLES AND STRATEGIES

Here are real-life examples of how effective communication can empower minority women in professional settings:

- **Scenario 1: Addressing Microaggressions**

  Imagine you're in a meeting, and a colleague comments on your hairstyle, implying it's "unprofessional." This remark may reflect a microaggression, rooted in unconscious bias about race and appearance. Instead of reacting defensively, you could respond calmly and assertively:

"I understand you're trying to be helpful, but I'd prefer if we stayed focused on the discussion. My hairstyle doesn't affect my ability to contribute to this project."

- **Scenario 2: Advocating for a Promotion**

  You've consistently exceeded expectations in your role, but you're overlooked for a promotion. Believing unconscious bias may have influenced the decision, you decide to address it professionally by speaking with your manager:

"I'm disappointed to hear I wasn't selected for the promotion. I'm deeply invested in my growth within this company and would appreciate your feedback to help me continue improving."

BUILDING CONFIDENCE IN COMMUNICATION

Confidence in communication develops through consistent practice and trust in your abilities. Here are strategies to help you communicate with confidence:

1. **Practice Public Speaking:** Consider joining a Toastmasters group or enrolling in a public speaking course to refine your presentation skills.
2. **Engage in Role-playing and Mock Interviews:** Rehearse challenging conversations with a trusted

friend or mentor to improve your delivery and adaptability.

3. **Incorporate Affirmations and Visualization:** Reinforce your positive self-image with affirmations and imagine yourself communicating effectively in various scenarios.

4. **Request Constructive Feedback:** Seek insights from trusted colleagues or mentors to identify areas of strength and opportunities for improvement.

5. **Embrace Your Unique Voice:** Stay authentic to your personality and communication style—being true to yourself enhances credibility and connection.

THE IMPORTANCE OF EMPATHY

Empathy is an essential component of effective communication, particularly for minority women. It enables you to connect with others on a meaningful level, establish trust, and handle challenging conversations with care and understanding.

- **Active Listening:** Focus on genuinely understanding the perspectives and emotions of others without interrupting or formulating a response prematurely.

- **Nonverbal Communication:** Observe others' nonverbal cues to better gauge their emotions and reactions.
- **Perspective-Taking:** Strive to understand situations from another person's viewpoint, even if you don't fully agree with their perspective.

CULTIVATING A SUPPORTIVE NETWORK

Building a network of supportive allies is key to navigating challenges in the workplace. Here are some steps to foster a positive and empowering environment:

- **Mentorship and Sponsorship:** Identify mentors who can provide guidance and encouragement, and consider mentoring others to pay it forward.
- **Professional Networks:** Join industry organizations and online communities to connect with like-minded professionals and share opportunities.
- **Allyship and Advocacy:** Collaborate with individuals who actively champion diversity and inclusion.
- **Collaboration Over Competition:** Prioritize relationships that promote teamwork and collective success over rivalry.

CONCLUSION

Improving communication skills is a continuous process that requires commitment, practice, and openness to growth. By adopting effective strategies, minority women can overcome biases, build trust, and create meaningful change within their organizations and communities.

As you refine your communication skills, stay authentic, confident, and empathetic. Your voice is powerful, and your story deserves to be heard.

BUILDING CONFIDENCE AS A LEADER

Imagine you're standing on the brink of a leadership role, your heart racing with a mix of excitement and apprehension. You've worked tirelessly to reach this point, yet the weight of expectations, the fear of imposter syndrome, and the societal pressures you face as a minority woman may make you question your readiness. But take heart—confidence, like any skill, can be nurtured and developed. This chapter will provide you with the tools and strategies to radiate confidence, lead with authenticity, and inspire your team to achieve new levels of success.

Confidence isn't about pretending to have it all together; it's about embracing your strengths, acknowledging areas for growth, and leveraging your unique experiences to craft a leadership style that is both impactful and authentic. It's about trusting in yourself, your abilities, and your vision, even in the face of challenges or resistance.

Think of confidence as a multidimensional concept composed of various key elements. One essential component is **self-awareness.** This involves evaluating your strengths and weaknesses with honesty, recognizing your unique value, and understanding your leadership style. Are you a natural collaborator or a decisive decision-maker? Do you excel at motivating teams or creating long-term strategies? By identifying your core competencies, you can harness them to inspire and lead effectively.

Another critical element is **self-belief.** This means acknowledging your achievements, celebrating your milestones, and cultivating a positive self-image. When you believe in yourself, you create an environment where others are inspired to believe in you as well. It's natural to feel moments of self-doubt, especially when navigating a predominantly white, male-dominated corporate landscape. However, it's essential to remember that your unique journey, resilience, and dedication to excellence have earned you this opportunity. Embrace your story and let it be the foundation of your confidence.

BUILDING CONFIDENCE THROUGH ACTION

Confidence isn't just a feeling—it's the result of consistent action. Here are practical strategies to help you develop and project confidence in your leadership role:

1. **Practice Active Listening:** Effective leaders don't just speak; they listen attentively. Focus on your team members' perspectives, engage in meaningful conversations, and demonstrate genuine respect and empathy. This creates an inclusive environment where everyone feels valued and heard.

2. **Enhance Your Communication Skills:** Clear and impactful communication is essential for effective leadership. Refine your ability to articulate your vision, inspire your team, and provide constructive feedback. Practice presenting your ideas confidently, using purposeful body language and maintaining eye contact to reinforce your message.

3. **Seek Mentorship and Sponsorship:** Build relationships with mentors who can provide guidance, challenge your thinking, and support your growth. Additionally, seek sponsors who can advocate for your advancement and connect you with new opportunities.

4. **View Mistakes as Learning Opportunities:** No leader is without flaws. Instead of fearing mistakes,

treat them as opportunities for growth. Reflect on your experiences, adapt your strategies, and emerge stronger with each lesson learned.

5. **Celebrate Wins, Big and Small:** Recognize your team's achievements and take time to celebrate both individual and collective successes. This reinforces positive actions, boosts morale, and fosters a culture of appreciation.
6. **Maintain a Professional Presence:** Present yourself in a manner that reflects your commitment to your leadership role. Dress appropriately for your position and maintain a professional demeanor. This reassures your team and stakeholders of your dedication and readiness.

NAVIGATING CHALLENGES WITH CONFIDENCE

As a minority woman in leadership, you will inevitably face unique challenges, including microaggressions, unconscious bias, navigating corporate politics, and managing difficult personalities. Here are strategies to navigate these obstacles with confidence:

1. Respond to Microaggressions with Grace:

Microaggressions can undermine your confidence and sense of belonging. Developing effective strategies to handle them is crucial. When confronted with a microaggression, strive to remain calm and composed. Address the behavior directly by calmly explaining why it is inappropriate and hurtful.

2. Challenge Implicit Bias:

Take a proactive stance against implicit bias in your workplace. Educate colleagues about its impact and advocate for initiatives that promote diversity and inclusion.

3. Use Your Voice to Advocate for Others:

Stand up for colleagues experiencing discrimination or unfair treatment. Your voice can serve as a catalyst for positive change, contributing to a more equitable workplace.

4. Build Strong Networks:

Connect with other minority women in leadership roles to gain mentorship, support, and a sense of community. Building these relationships can provide invaluable guidance and solidarity.

DEVELOPING A LEADERSHIP STYLE THAT RESONATES

Your leadership style should reflect your authentic self. It's not about mimicking others but about embracing your unique qualities and strengths.

1. **Embrace Your Strengths:** Identify your natural talents and abilities, and use them to inspire and motivate your team. Are you a strong communicator, a visionary thinker, or a skilled strategist? Leverage these strengths to shape a leadership style that feels genuine to you.
2. **Cultivate Emotional Intelligence:** Strengthen your emotional intelligence to understand yourself and others better. This helps you build meaningful relationships, manage conflicts effectively, and foster a supportive work environment.

PROJECTING CONFIDENCE WITH BODY LANGUAGE

Your body language can powerfully convey your confidence. Here are key aspects to consider:

1. **Maintain Eye Contact:** Making eye contact demonstrates that you are confident and fully engaged in the conversation.

2. **Use Open Body Language:** Adopt an open posture, relaxed stance, and a slight smile to signal confidence and approachability.
3. **Speak with Conviction:** The tone and cadence of your voice matter. Speak clearly, at a deliberate pace, and with assurance.
4. **Dress for Success:** Wear attire appropriate for your role, ensuring it reflects your professionalism and confidence.

CONFIDENCE IS A JOURNEY, NOT A DESTINATION

Building confidence is an ongoing process, requiring commitment, self-reflection, and a willingness to grow. View challenges as opportunities for development, celebrate your achievements, and remain steadfast in your belief in your ability to lead authentically and effectively.

The path to confident leadership may be demanding, but its rewards are profound. With each step you take, you empower yourself and inspire others to strive for their own success.

MENTORSHIP AND SPONSORSHIP

The journey to leadership is rarely one you take alone. While confidence and skills are essential, having mentors and sponsors who advocate for your growth can be transformative. These relationships provide invaluable guidance, support, and access to opportunities that can accelerate your career and help you achieve your goals.

Imagine this: you're a rising star in your field, full of talent and ambition. You've already achieved notable successes, but now you're at a crossroads—a challenging project, a tough negotiation, or a career shift that feels overwhelming. This is where mentorship and sponsorship become crucial. They act as a compass, helping you navigate complexities and opening doors to opportunities you might not have discovered on your own.

THE POWER OF MENTORSHIP

Mentorship is like having a trusted advisor by your side. It's a relationship where an experienced individual, the mentor, provides guidance and support to someone less experienced, the mentee. Mentors can come from various backgrounds—they might be a colleague, a senior leader, a professor, or someone you've met through a professional network. They share valuable insights from their own experiences, helping you overcome challenges, refine your skills, and build confidence in your abilities.

Mentorship is a two-way street. While you gain essential guidance and support, you also bring fresh ideas and enthusiasm to the relationship. This reciprocal exchange fosters a dynamic learning environment that enriches both you and your mentor.

SEEKING A MENTOR: FINDING YOUR GUIDING LIGHT

Finding a mentor is an active process that requires intentional effort. It's not about waiting for someone to appear—it's about seeking out individuals who can help you grow and thrive in your career.

1. **Identify Your Needs:** Reflect on your career goals and the areas where you need guidance. What skills do you want to develop? What specific challenges are you facing? Having clarity on these points will help you identify the right mentor.
2. **Network and Connect:** Participate in professional events, attend industry conferences, join relevant organizations, and leverage platforms like LinkedIn to connect with potential mentors.

3. **Reach Out with Purpose:** When you've identified individuals who inspire you, reach out with a clear and personalized message. Express admiration for their work, share your goals, and explain how their guidance could benefit your development.
4. **Develop a Mentorship Plan:** Once you establish a connection, set clear expectations for the relationship. Discuss how often you'll meet, what topics you'll cover, and how you'll measure progress together.

THE ART OF MENTORSHIP: SHARING YOUR KNOWLEDGE

As you advance in your career, mentoring others becomes an opportunity to give back, strengthen your leadership skills, and leave a lasting impact.

1. **Be a Supportive Listener:** Create a safe and non-judgmental space for your mentee to share their challenges, experiences, and aspirations.
2. **Provide Guidance and Feedback:** Offer insights and advice, but focus on guiding rather than directing. Share constructive feedback to help your mentee grow and make informed decisions.
3. **Encourage and Empower:** Celebrate your mentee's successes and provide support during setbacks.

Empower them to take ownership of their development and career path.

BEYOND MENTORSHIP: THE POWER OF SPONSORSHIP

While mentorship provides guidance, sponsorship takes a more active role in advocating for your career progression. A sponsor is a senior individual who champions your advancement, opens doors to new opportunities, and uses their influence to support your success.

FINDING A SPONSOR: BUILDING RELATIONSHIPS WITH INFLUENCERS

Building sponsorship relationships requires cultivating strong connections with influential individuals in your field.

1. **Identify Influencers:** Look for senior leaders, industry experts, or individuals in your network with significant influence and a willingness to support rising talent.
2. **Demonstrate Your Value:** Showcase your unique contributions by consistently delivering high-quality work and exceeding expectations.
3. **Cultivate Relationships:** Build genuine connections by engaging in meaningful conversations, seeking

their guidance, and demonstrating your commitment to learning and growth.

4. **Seek Out Opportunities:** Be proactive in showcasing your skills and aspirations. Express interest in taking on new challenges and share your career goals with potential sponsors.

SPONSORING OTHERS: CHAMPIONING FUTURE LEADERS

As you advance in your career, you can play a pivotal role as a sponsor by supporting the next generation of leaders.

1. **Recognize Potential:** Identify individuals with the talent, drive, and potential to make meaningful contributions.

2. **Invest in Their Growth:** Go beyond offering advice by providing opportunities for skill development, challenging projects, and increased visibility within the organization.

3. **Be a Vocal Advocate:** Actively promote their work, highlight their achievements, and speak positively about their contributions to key stakeholders.

4. **Open Doors to Opportunities:** Use your influence to connect them with decision-makers and create pathways for their career advancement.

THE POWER OF A NETWORK OF MENTORS AND SPONSORS

Building a network of mentors and sponsors is one of the most effective ways to develop as a leader. This network provides invaluable support, guidance, and access to opportunities that can shape your career and broaden your impact.

1. **Diverse Perspectives:** A network that includes mentors and sponsors from different backgrounds and experiences enriches your professional growth by offering a wide range of perspectives.
2. **Amplified Influence:** Having multiple advocates strengthens your voice and enhances your visibility within your organization and industry.
3. **Lifelong Learning:** Mentors and sponsors can provide guidance and encouragement throughout your career, supporting ongoing learning and development.

NAVIGATING CHALLENGES

While building a network of mentors and sponsors is rewarding, it's not without its challenges. Here are some common obstacles and strategies to overcome them:

1. **Finding the Right Fit:** Not every mentor or sponsor will align perfectly with your needs. Be open to exploring various connections until you find individuals who genuinely support your growth.
2. **Avoiding Overdependence:** While mentorship and sponsorship are valuable, maintaining your independence is crucial. Take ownership of your career by developing your skills and seeking opportunities to grow on your own.
3. **Navigating Power Dynamics:** Recognize that mentors and sponsors may hold different levels of influence within your organization. While respecting their positions, confidently advocate for your needs and aspirations.

A LEGACY OF LEADERSHIP

Mentorship and sponsorship are not only tools for career advancement—they are about creating a legacy of leadership. By guiding and supporting others, you inspire the next generation of leaders and contribute to a culture of collaboration and inclusion.

EMBRACE THE POWER OF MENTORSHIP AND SPONSORSHIP

Mentorship and sponsorship are transformative forces on your career journey. By seeking guidance, support, and advocacy, you chart a course for success. At the same time, you have the opportunity to give back by mentoring and sponsoring others, creating a ripple effect of positive change.

As you navigate your career, remember the incredible value of cultivating a network of mentors and sponsors. This network will not only fuel your growth but also help build a more inclusive and supportive professional environment for all.

LEADING WITH EMPATHY

Empathy—the ability to understand and share the feelings of others—is not just a soft skill. It is a powerful tool that can transform leadership and team building. Empathy is the foundation for building trust, enhancing collaboration, and fostering a truly inclusive work environment. This is especially vital for minority women who navigate the complexities of corporate culture.

Imagine a workplace where employees feel heard, understood, and appreciated for their unique perspectives. Leadership in such an environment goes beyond listening to feedback; it involves understanding the emotions and experiences behind those perspectives. Empathy strengthens relationships and lays the groundwork for high-performing, inclusive teams.

EMPATHY AS A LEADERSHIP COMPASS

In leadership, empathy serves as a guiding principle. When leaders take the time to understand their team members' struggles, aspirations, and needs, they can tailor their support accordingly. This includes offering mentorship, addressing challenges, and creating growth opportunities that align with individual goals.

Empathy isn't about reading minds—it's about cultivating attentiveness and receptiveness. It involves:

- Actively listening to what is said and unsaid.
- Paying attention to verbal and nonverbal cues.
- Asking thoughtful questions to better understand the situation.

By demonstrating genuine interest, leaders build trust and create an environment where everyone feels safe to share their ideas and perspectives.

EMPATHY IN ACTION: ADDRESSING WORKPLACE CHALLENGES

Empathy is particularly impactful in addressing issues faced by minority women in the workplace:

1. **Addressing Microaggressions:** Subtle, often unintentional acts of bias—microaggressions—can leave minority women feeling marginalized. An empathetic leader recognizes these experiences, provides a safe space for discussion, and fosters a culture where these discriminatory behaviors are acknowledged and addressed.
2. **Navigating Tokenism:** Tokenism, where efforts to include minorities are seen as symbolic rather than substantive, can lead to feelings of isolation. Empathetic leaders actively address these challenges by creating a workplace where individuals are valued for their contributions, not just their demographics.
3. **Creating a Supportive Environment:** In predominantly white, male-dominated workplaces, the absence of role models can be a significant barrier for minority women. Empathetic leaders bridge this gap by establishing mentorship programs and connecting

minority women with mentors who can provide guidance, support, and community.

Beyond individual interactions, empathy promotes a culture of inclusivity. By listening to and valuing diverse perspectives, empathetic leaders create an environment where collaboration flourishes, and everyone feels appreciated.

PRACTICAL TIPS FOR CULTIVATING EMPATHY IN LEADERSHIP

1. **Active Listening:** Pay attention to both verbal and nonverbal cues. Look for subtle signs of discomfort, frustration, or disengagement and address them promptly.
2. **Empathetic Communication:** Use language that reflects understanding and compassion. Avoid making assumptions or judgments; instead, ask open-ended questions to encourage dialogue.
3. **Perspective-Taking:** Consider situations from your team members' perspectives. Factor in their cultural backgrounds, personal experiences, and unique challenges.
4. **Emotional Intelligence:** Develop self-awareness by understanding your own emotions and learning to

recognize and manage the emotions of others effectively.

5. **Feedback and Open Communication:** Foster a culture where team members feel comfortable sharing feedback and voicing concerns without fear of judgment.

6. **Mentorship and Support:** Actively seek opportunities to mentor minority women. Provide guidance, encouragement, and tools to help them navigate workplace challenges.

EMPATHY: A CORNERSTONE OF LEADERSHIP

Empathy is not about pity; it is about understanding perspectives, valuing experiences, and using that knowledge to create a supportive and inclusive environment. Leaders who prioritize empathy unlock their team's potential, creating a more equitable and thriving workplace. By embracing empathy, you can empower your team and drive meaningful change in your organization.

CHAPTER 3

FINANCIAL EMPOWERMENT

UNDERSTANDING FINANCIAL LITERACY

Imagine a world where you, a minority woman, are equipped with the knowledge and tools to navigate finances confidently. A world where you understand the essentials of budgeting, investing, and building lasting wealth. This world is attainable, and it begins with understanding financial literacy.

Financial literacy is the cornerstone of financial well-being. It's about acquiring the knowledge and skills needed to manage your money effectively, make sound decisions, and achieve your goals. For minority women, who often face distinct challenges, becoming financially literate is especially important.

Picture yourself as a young woman just starting your career. You're thrilled about your new job but also anxious about managing your finances. You're aware of the systemic inequalities that could make it harder to accumulate wealth compared to others. How can you navigate these hurdles effectively?

This is where financial literacy becomes transformative. It's not only about understanding numbers; it's about empowering yourself with the knowledge to take charge of your financial journey. It includes understanding budgeting, saving, investing, managing debt, and credit scores. It's about breaking down the misconceptions that can prevent financial progress, particularly for minority women.

For example, you may have heard that investing is too risky or complex or that borrowing money signifies failure. These ideas can discourage minority women from taking an active role in their finances. Financial literacy challenges these beliefs and provides the confidence to make informed decisions.

Let's explore the essential aspects of financial literacy and how they can help you take control of your finances. Regardless of your age or current situation, it's never too late to start learning.

UNDERSTANDING BUDGETING

Budgeting is the practice of planning how you'll spend and save. It's a way to create a plan for your money, ensuring you're using it wisely and directing it toward your goals. Think of it as a roadmap guiding your financial journey and helping you stay on course.

For minority women, budgeting may involve navigating additional responsibilities like supporting extended family, meeting cultural expectations, or handling costs associated with childcare and healthcare. Creating a realistic budget tailored to your unique circumstances is essential. Begin by identifying your income and expenses, then set financial goals that align with your aspirations.

SAVING FOR THE FUTURE

Saving is essential for financial stability. Setting aside a portion of your income regularly creates a financial safety net for unexpected situations and helps you achieve long-term goals.

Imagine facing an unexpected medical bill, car repair, or job loss. Without savings, such events can cause significant stress. However, a well-thought-out savings plan can help you navigate these challenges with greater resilience. Saving also helps you achieve milestones like purchasing a home, funding education, or retiring comfortably. Reflect on your financial aspirations and make saving a priority.

THE POWER OF INVESTING

Investing involves putting your money to work, allowing it to grow over time. It utilizes the principle of compounding, where the returns on your investments generate additional returns, creating a consistent pattern of growth.

For minority women, investing is an essential strategy for building and passing wealth to future generations. It's about gaining control over your financial journey and establishing a secure future for yourself and your loved ones.

DEBT MANAGEMENT: A BALANCING ACT

Debt is a common part of financial life, but managing it effectively is key to preventing it from becoming overwhelming. This requires understanding different types of debt, such as student loans, credit card balances, and personal loans, and implementing strategies to pay them down systematically.

Remember, debt can be a resource for building credit and achieving significant milestones, but it's important to stay mindful of interest rates and repayment terms. Avoid accumulating unnecessary debt, and focus on reducing it in a planned, deliberate manner.

Credit Scores: Your Financial Footprint

Your credit score is a numerical measure of your ability to manage debt responsibly. It plays a critical role in obtaining loans, credit cards, mortgages, and even securing rental agreements.

Building a strong credit score is fundamental to your financial health. Make timely payments, handle credit wisely, and maintain a balanced mix of credit accounts to steadily improve your score over time.

OVERCOMING FINANCIAL BARRIERS

Minority women often encounter specific financial obstacles that can impede their progress toward financial stability. These challenges include:

- **Lower Average Income:**
  Pay disparities based on race and gender can significantly affect a woman's earning capacity, making it harder to accumulate savings or invest.
- **Limited Access to Financial Resources:**
  Many minority communities have reduced access to financial institutions, such as banks and credit unions. This limitation can restrict options for obtaining loans, opening accounts, or receiving sound financial advice.
- **Cultural and Societal Expectations:**
  Minority women may face societal pressures to provide financial support to extended family members or adhere to cultural norms that influence spending and saving habits.
- **Gaps in Financial Literacy:**
  Limited access to financial education and tools can make it harder for minority women to acquire the knowledge needed to make confident, well-informed financial decisions.

BREAKING THROUGH THE BARRIERS

Overcoming financial barriers requires a well-rounded approach. It's about taking initiative, being resourceful, and staying committed to your goals. Here are some strategies to tackle these challenges:

- **Seek Financial Education:**

  Attend workshops, read books, and explore online resources to gain practical knowledge about budgeting, saving, investing, and managing debt.

- **Connect with Financial Advisors:**

  Work with financial professionals to create customized plans tailored to your unique circumstances and goals.

- **Build a Support Network:**

  Surround yourself with individuals who understand your financial challenges and can provide encouragement, advice, and accountability.

- **Advocate for Financial Inclusion:**

  Support programs and organizations that promote financial literacy and empower minority women to achieve lasting financial security.

FINANCIAL LITERACY AS A TOOL FOR EMPOWERMENT

Financial literacy is more than just managing money—it's about equipping yourself with the knowledge and skills to take control of your financial future. It's about making informed choices, creating opportunities, and establishing a stable foundation for yourself and your family.

Remember, your financial journey is uniquely yours. Embrace financial literacy as a tool for growth, resilience, and achieving personal goals. You possess the intelligence, determination, and strength to succeed in the financial world and build a brighter future with confidence.

BUDGETING FOR SUCCESS

Imagine a world where financial stability isn't a distant dream but a tangible reality, where your financial choices empower you to create the future you envision. This is the impact of budgeting—a skill that's not just about numbers but about taking control of your financial journey.

For minority women, financial empowerment carries even greater significance due to systemic challenges. From wage disparities to the responsibilities of caregiving, we often balance financial obligations with limited resources. However, adopting mindful budgeting practices can help overcome these barriers and open the door to financial independence.

THINK OF BUDGETING AS YOUR FINANCIAL GUIDE

Budgeting serves as a map for your financial journey. It directs you toward your goals, helps you avoid unnecessary detours, and ensures you're prepared for unexpected financial hurdles. It's not a rigid rulebook but a flexible framework tailored to your unique circumstances and aspirations.

UNDERSTANDING YOUR FINANCIAL SITUATION

Before exploring budgeting strategies, it's essential to have a clear picture of your current financial standing. This involves understanding your income, expenses, and overall financial health.

- **Income:** List all your income sources, such as salary, side hustles, investments, and other earnings. This establishes the foundation for your budget.
- **Expenses:** Track your spending over one or two months. Use a spreadsheet, budgeting app, or even a notebook to record every expenditure, from groceries to entertainment meticulously. Honesty about your spending habits is crucial for identifying areas to adjust.

- **Financial Health:** Assess your overall financial situation. Do you have outstanding debts? If so, what are the terms? Do you have savings? Understanding these details will help you set realistic financial goals.

CREATING A BUDGET THAT FITS YOUR LIFE

The next step is crafting a budget that aligns with your goals and lifestyle. Choose a budgeting method that works for you:

- **50/30/20 Rule:** Allocate 50% of your after-tax income to needs (housing, utilities, groceries), 30% to wants (entertainment, dining out), and 20% to savings or debt repayment.
- **Zero-Based Budget:** Assign every dollar of your income to a specific category, ensuring you spend within your means.
- **Envelope Method:** Allocate cash into physical envelopes for categories like groceries, gas, and entertainment. Spend only what's in the envelope for each category.

TIPS FOR SUCCESSFUL BUDGETING

Once you've chosen a budgeting strategy, these tips can help ensure success:

- **Monitor Your Progress:** Regularly review your budget to stay on track. Celebrate milestones and adjust as needed.
- **Automate Savings:** Schedule automatic transfers from your checking account to your savings account.
- **Negotiate Bills:** Don't hesitate to contact service providers to negotiate lower rates.
- **Seek Expert Help:** If creating or managing a budget feels overwhelming, consider consulting a financial advisor or counselor.

INVESTING: BUILDING WEALTH FOR THE FUTURE

While budgeting lays the groundwork for financial stability, investing can help grow your wealth over time.

- **Start Small:** Begin with manageable amounts—every little bit adds up over time.
- **Diversify:** Spread your investments across different asset types like stocks, bonds, and real estate to reduce risk.

- **Seek Advice:** If you're new to investing, work with a financial advisor for tailored guidance.

ADDRESSING FINANCIAL CHALLENGES

Minority women face unique financial obstacles, but these can be tackled effectively:

- **Wage Disparities:** Advocate for yourself by negotiating salaries and promoting equal pay in your workplace.
- **Caregiving Responsibilities:** Caring for family members can strain finances. Look for support systems and resources that ease the burden.
- **Access to Credit:** Building and maintaining good credit is essential. Make timely payments and use credit responsibly to improve your credit score.

BUILDING A FINANCIALLY SECURE FUTURE

Financial empowerment is about more than managing money—it's about creating a future you can control and be proud of. Budgeting is the first step toward this goal, offering a roadmap to stability and growth. By taking a mindful approach to your finances, you can achieve your dreams and establish a lasting legacy of financial success.

INVESTING WITH CONFIDENCE

Investing with confidence often begins with a mix of excitement and apprehension. For many minority women, the financial world can feel intimidating, filled with complex jargon and strategies that seem out of reach. But taking control of your financial future doesn't require expertise in Wall Street trading—it requires a willingness to learn, courage, and belief in your ability to make informed choices.

This chapter serves as your guide to navigating the investment world. It simplifies the process and offers practical steps to help you create a secure financial future. From foundational knowledge to advanced strategies, this chapter empowers you to make confident decisions with your money.

UNDERSTANDING THE BASICS: BUILDING A STRONG FOUNDATION

Investing means putting your money to work to generate returns over time. While the prospect of growing your wealth is appealing, understanding the basics is critical before taking the first step.

1. **Risk Tolerance:** Evaluate your comfort level with the possibility of loss. Are you more inclined toward stability or open to higher risks for potentially greater

returns? Your risk tolerance will influence your investment decisions.

2. **Investment Time Horizon:** Determine how long you plan to hold your investments. Short-term investments last a year or less, while long-term ones span several years or decades. A longer horizon allows investments to grow while buffering against short-term market fluctuations.

3. **Diversification:** Spread your investments across multiple asset classes like stocks, bonds, and real estate. Diversification reduces the impact of a single underperforming asset on your overall portfolio.

INVESTMENT OPTIONS: EXPLORING PATHWAYS TO FINANCIAL GROWTH

With a strong foundation in place, consider these common investment options:

1. **Stocks:** Owning stocks means owning part of a company. While stocks can be volatile, they offer significant long-term growth potential.
   - Individual Stocks: Investing in individual companies requires research into their financial health and industry outlook.

- Mutual Funds: Mutual funds pool resources from multiple investors to buy a variety of stocks, providing diversification without extensive research.
- Exchange-Traded Funds (ETFs): ETFs are traded like individual stocks but offer diversification and cost-effectiveness.

2. **Bonds:** Bonds involve lending money to governments or corporations in exchange for interest payments. They typically carry lower risks than stocks.
   - **Corporate Bonds:** Issued by businesses.
   - **Government Bonds:** Issued by governments, often considered safer investments.

3. **Real Estate:** Real estate can generate income through rentals or appreciate over time. Options include direct property investments or Real Estate Investment Trusts (REITs).

4. **Commodities:** Commodities like oil, gold, and agricultural products offer diversification and can act as a hedge against inflation.

SEEKING GUIDANCE: MAKING INFORMED DECISIONS

The investment world can feel overwhelming, especially for beginners. Professional guidance can simplify the process:

- **Financial Advisors:** Advisors tailor investment plans to your goals, risk tolerance, and time horizon.
- **Robo-Advisors:** Online platforms use algorithms to manage investments based on your preferences, offering cost-effective and automated solutions.
- **Online Investment Platforms:** Tools like Robinhood or Acorns make investing accessible, offering options for stocks, ETFs, and fractional shares.

FINANCIAL LITERACY: THE FOUNDATION OF SUCCESS

Building financial literacy is key to confident investing. It encompasses understanding budgeting, saving, and money management.

1. **Budgeting:** Budgeting tracks your income and expenses, identifies savings opportunities, and supports financial goals.

2. **Saving:** Saving creates the funds you'll use for investing, allowing you to grow your money over time.
3. **Emergency Funds:** A safety net for unforeseen expenses, an emergency fund prevents financial setbacks during crises.

OVERCOMING BARRIERS: EMPOWERING MINORITY WOMEN

Minority women often face unique financial challenges, including:

1. **Limited Resources:** Restricted financial resources can make investing seem out of reach.
2. **Fear of Failure:** Concerns about making mistakes can hinder confidence. Remember, mistakes are learning opportunities.
3. **Lack of Access:** Limited access to financial education can create obstacles to informed decision-making.
4. **Societal Pressures:** Balancing personal goals with familial expectations can impact financial priorities.
5. **Systemic Bias:** Discrimination in the financial system disproportionately affects minority women.

STRATEGIES FOR BREAKING THROUGH BARRIERS

1. **Start Small:** Begin with manageable amounts and increase investments as confidence grows.
2. **Seek Knowledge:** Learn about investment strategies through books, courses, and seminars.
3. **Join Support Networks:** Connect with others navigating similar journeys to share advice and encouragement.
4. **Advocate for Yourself:** Ask questions and seek help from financial professionals.
5. **Find Mentors:** Build relationships with experienced women in finance for guidance and inspiration.

YOUR UNIQUE PATH TO FINANCIAL GROWTH

Investing with confidence requires knowledge and trust in your ability to make sound choices. By understanding the basics, exploring options, seeking advice, and overcoming obstacles, you can empower yourself to create a secure financial future. Remember, there's no one-size-fits-all approach—embrace your unique journey, stay focused on your goals, and watch your investments thrive over time

OVERCOMING FINANCIAL BARRIERS

The journey to financial empowerment for minority women is often marked by unique challenges. These barriers can arise from systemic inequalities, historical disadvantages, and societal expectations that restrict access to opportunities and resources. However, these challenges are not insurmountable. By understanding and addressing financial barriers, we can empower minority women to take control of their financial future and achieve meaningful progress.

THE DEBT CYCLE

One major financial barrier faced by minority women is the persistent cycle of debt. This cycle is often driven by factors such as lower starting salaries, limited access to affordable housing, and the disproportionate burden of family care. The strain of student loans, medical expenses, and daily living costs can lead to overwhelming financial pressure.

Consider Jasmine, a single mother working two jobs to stay afloat. She constantly juggles bills, making it difficult to save for emergencies or invest in her future. High interest rates on her student loans and credit cards compound her financial struggles, trapping her in a cycle of debt. Jasmine's story is a common one, reflecting the challenges faced by many minority women striving to build financial stability and security.

LIMITED ACCESS TO CREDIT

The lack of access to affordable credit is another significant hurdle for minority women. Banks and financial institutions often assess creditworthiness using criteria that disadvantage minority communities, such as limited credit history, lower credit scores, and fewer financial resources. These factors can hinder efforts to secure loans, mortgages, and other financial tools, restricting opportunities to buy homes, start businesses, or pursue higher education.

Take Londyn, a young entrepreneur who dreams of opening her own bakery. Despite her dedication and solid business plan, she struggles to secure a loan from traditional lenders due to her limited credit history. This lack of access to capital stalls her dream of financial independence and business success.

FINANCIAL LITERACY GAP

The financial literacy gap is a significant barrier to empowerment for minority women. Limited access to financial education, cultural attitudes toward money management, and minimal guidance from family and communities often contribute to this gap.

For instance, Jessica, a recent college graduate, struggles with understanding basic financial concepts. She is unfamiliar with the differences between saving and investing, how to create a budget, or how to manage credit effectively. Without this foundational knowledge, she finds it challenging to make informed financial decisions and reach her goals.

DISCRIMINATION IN THE WORKPLACE

Workplace discrimination also plays a critical role in the financial challenges faced by minority women. Unequal pay, limited opportunities for promotions, and insufficient access to professional development resources contribute to lower earnings and greater financial insecurity.

Angela's story illustrates this point. Despite being a highly skilled professional in a male-dominated industry, she earns less than her male counterparts for the same work. This inequity not only impacts her current financial situation but also limits her long-term earning potential and economic mobility.

THE POWER OF FINANCIAL EMPOWERMENT

Addressing these financial barriers is essential for minority women to achieve economic independence. By recognizing the systemic inequalities at play, we can develop strategies that empower individuals and foster lasting change.

STRATEGIES FOR OVERCOMING FINANCIAL BARRIERS

- **Financial Education**: Gaining access to financial education is crucial. Resources such as online courses, workshops, and community programs can help minority women build their understanding of budgeting, saving, investing, and managing credit effectively.
- **Building Credit History**: Establishing and maintaining a good credit history is essential for accessing financial resources. Timely bill payments and responsible credit use can improve credit scores, enabling access to better financial opportunities.
- **Negotiating for Fair Pay**: Advocating for equitable compensation is vital. Researching industry standards, understanding personal worth,

and confidently negotiating can help close the pay gap.

- **Seeking Financial Guidance**: Connecting with financial advisors, mentors, and support networks can provide essential advice and resources for financial growth and stability.
- **Exploring Alternative Financing Options**: Community development financial institutions (CDFIs) and credit unions often offer flexible financial solutions that may not be available from traditional banks.
- **Investing for the Future:** Learning about investment options and developing a personalized investment plan can pave the way for long-term wealth and financial security.
- **Building a Support System:** A strong network of friends, family, and mentors provides emotional and practical support during financial challenges.

BREAKING THE CYCLE

Overcoming financial barriers involves more than individual responsibility—it requires systemic change. Advocacy for fair lending practices, equitable pay, and accessible financial education programs is essential to dismantling the inequalities that perpetuate these challenges.

By equipping minority women with the tools to manage their finances effectively, we build not only individual success stories but also a more inclusive and prosperous society. Financial empowerment is a collective journey, requiring individuals to take proactive steps while advocating for systemic changes that create a fairer playing field. Through education, advocacy, and collaborative efforts, we can eliminate financial barriers and shape a brighter future for all minority women.

CREATING MULTIPLE INCOME STREAMS

Financial security isn't just about having a steady job—it's about creating diverse sources of income to ensure your financial future is resilient and adaptable. For many minority women, this can feel like an uphill battle, navigating systems that seem to confine them to a single paycheck. But imagine this: instead of relying on just one income source, you cultivate multiple streams, each contributing to your financial stability and peace of mind. This approach helps build a safety net that can weather unexpected challenges.

If one source of income slows or disappears, others can sustain you. Diversifying income is a powerful strategy to take control of your financial future and build a life that's truly secure.

There are countless ways to establish multiple income streams. Some require initial investments of time and money, while others can be launched with minimal resources. The key is finding a balance that aligns with your personal goals and financial circumstances.

PROVEN METHODS FOR CREATING MULTIPLE INCOME STREAMS

1. Side Hustles and Freelancing

- **Turning Passions into Income:** Do you have a skill or passion that could generate revenue? Whether you're an excellent baker, a talented artist, or a skilled writer, platforms like Etsy, Fiverr, and Upwork make it easier than ever to monetize your talents.
- **Sharing Your Expertise:** If you have specialized knowledge, consider offering consulting, coaching, or workshops. These services can be provided in person or online, allowing you to earn extra income while sharing your expertise.

- **Participating in the Gig Economy:** The gig economy has expanded rapidly, offering flexible opportunities across industries. From ride-sharing services to food delivery, you can explore various options to earn additional income on your own schedule.

2. **Investing in Your Future**
    - **Gaining Financial Knowledge:** Investing in financial education is foundational. Understanding budgeting, saving, and investment strategies empowers you to make smart decisions and build long-term financial security.
    - **Exploring Stock Market Opportunities:** While intimidating at first, stock market investing can be a valuable tool for wealth creation. Begin with small investments, learn about strategies, and gradually grow your portfolio.
    - **Real Estate:** A Tangible Investment: Real estate can offer passive income and appreciation over time. Consider options like buying rental properties or investing in Real Estate Investment Trusts (REITs).

3. **Starting Your Own Business**
   - **From Ideas to Reality:** If you have a business idea or a unique product to offer, starting your own business could be both rewarding and lucrative.
   - **Leveraging Online Tools:** The internet has made entrepreneurship more accessible. Launch an online store, offer digital products, or use social media to build a brand.
   - **Networking for Success:** Connecting with entrepreneurs, investors, and industry professionals can provide valuable insights and support as you grow your business.

NAVIGATING CHALLENGES

While building multiple income streams has many advantages, it also comes with challenges:
- Managing Your Time: Balancing a primary job, side hustles, and personal responsibilities requires effective time management. Planning and prioritizing tasks is essential.
- Practicing Financial Discipline: Keep track of your earnings and expenses. Focus on saving, investing, and managing any debt to avoid financial pitfalls.

- Overcoming Self-Doubt: Starting new ventures can be intimidating. Trust in your abilities, pursue your passions, and stay persistent through setbacks.

BUILDING A SUSTAINABLE FUTURE

Creating multiple income streams isn't just about financial security—it's about designing a fulfilling and sustainable life. It offers the freedom to pursue your passions, take control of your time, and shape a future aligned with your values.

Remember, this journey is ongoing. Building a diverse income portfolio requires effort, learning, and dedication to financial growth.

THE PATH TO FINANCIAL EMPOWERMENT

- **Adopt a Growth Mindset:** Stay open to new opportunities and challenges.
- **Prioritize Financial Education**: Continuously enhance your understanding of money management, investing, and entrepreneurship.
- **Build a Support System:** Surround yourself with individuals who inspire and encourage you.
- **Celebrate Your Progress**: Recognize and appreciate each milestone along the way.

Your journey to financial empowerment is uniquely yours. Embrace your strengths, learn from experiences, and trust in your ability to achieve your financial goals. This is your moment to create a secure, fulfilling, and purposeful future.

CHAPTER 4

BUILDING MEANINGFUL ALLIANCES

NETWORKING WITH PURPOSE

Networking isn't just about exchanging business cards—it's about forming authentic connections and building relationships that support your growth and amplify your voice. In a world where opportunities often arise through personal connections, building meaningful alliances is especially crucial for minority women who face unique challenges in professional spaces.

This is where "networking with purpose" becomes essential.

Imagine walking into a conference, career fair, or casual networking event. How can you make the most of these opportunities? The key isn't attending every event but showing up with a clear objective.

1. Define Your Goals

Before stepping into a networking setting, clarify your purpose. What are you looking for? Are you seeking mentorship, potential collaborators, industry insights, or simply expanding your professional circle? Having a clear goal allows you to focus your energy and make strategic connections.

For example, if your goal is to connect with mentors in the tech industry, start by identifying events where prominent tech leaders will be present. Research their profiles beforehand, prepare thoughtful questions, and align your goals with their expertise.

2. Cultivate a Growth Mindset

Networking is about building relationships that benefit both parties, not just extracting value for yourself. Approach each interaction with genuine curiosity. Ask open-ended questions, actively listen, and connect authentically with others' stories.

For instance, instead of simply asking someone about their job, ask about their career journey, what motivates them, or the challenges they've overcome. These deeper conversations foster trust and create meaningful connections.

3. Seek Allies and Mentors

Networking isn't only about finding connections—it's about identifying allies and mentors who can guide you along your journey.

Mentors offer support, advice, and insights, while allies can advocate for you and champion your growth. This doesn't always require formal mentorship programs. Your mentor might be a senior colleague, a peer who inspires you, or someone in your network who shares similar goals and aspirations.

4. Harness the Power of Storytelling

Your personal journey is one of your most valuable assets when networking. Sharing your experiences, resilience, and unique perspective helps others understand and relate to you.

Imagine being asked, "What's your story?" at an event. Use this opportunity to share how you've navigated challenges, overcome obstacles, and shaped your career aspirations. This approach fosters empathy and builds connections on a deeper level.

5. Build Trust Through Reciprocity

Networking isn't just about asking for help—it's about offering value to others. Think about how you can contribute to your network. Share your knowledge, connect people, offer support, or be a sounding board for ideas.

For example, if you're skilled at problem-solving or communication, offer your expertise to others in need. A reciprocal approach strengthens relationships and creates a sense of shared benefit.

6. Utilize Online Platforms

In today's digital era, online networking is as crucial as face-to-face interactions. Platforms like LinkedIn enable you to connect with professionals, expand your reach, and find mentors.

Build a strong online presence by showcasing your skills and accomplishments. Engage in conversations, share valuable content, and participate in relevant professional groups.

7. Be Consistent and Follow Up

Networking is an ongoing process, not a one-time event. Maintain contact with your network by following up after meetings, sending thank-you notes, or sharing useful articles. These small gestures build long-lasting relationships.

Remember, building meaningful alliances takes time, effort, and genuine commitment.

NAVIGATING THE NETWORKING LANDSCAPE AS A MINORITY WOMAN

For minority women, networking can come with unique challenges, such as implicit biases, lack of representation, or feelings of being "othered." However, these challenges can be overcome with strategic approaches and a strong sense of self.

1. Embrace Your Identity

Authenticity is your strength. Share your experiences openly—they can build empathy, foster understanding, and create stronger connections.

2. Seek Inclusive Networks

Look for organizations and events that prioritize diversity and inclusion. These spaces provide a supportive environment to connect with others who share your experiences.

3. Lean on Your Support System

Connect with family, friends, and fellow minority women for advice, encouragement, and support.

4. Be Patient and Persistent

Building a network takes time. Don't be discouraged by slow progress—keep attending events, engaging in conversations, and nurturing relationships.

BUILDING LASTING ALLIANCES

Networking with purpose is a journey, not a destination. Meaningful alliances are built on mutual respect, shared support, and a commitment to growth.

This network becomes your village, your support system, and your inspiration. It's the group that believes in your potential and cheers you on toward success. Remember, when you uplift others, you elevate yourself. Together, we can create a world where minority women are empowered to lead, thrive, and succeed.

COLLABORATION OVER COMPETITION

Imagine a workplace where competition isn't the sole driving force, but collaboration takes center stage. Picture an environment where shared success is the ultimate goal, and women of color support each other's growth by leveraging their collective strengths.

In this collaborative space, the focus shifts from individual achievement to collective advancement. The idea is simple yet powerful: we rise higher when we lift each other. This approach nurtures mutual growth and empowerment, creating opportunities that benefit everyone involved.

Think of it as an orchestra, where each musician contributes their unique talents to produce a harmonious symphony. Each woman in this network brings her own perspective, skills, and experiences. By working together, they amplify their collective impact, surpassing individual goals and creating something extraordinary.

PRACTICAL STEPS TO CULTIVATE COLLABORATION

1. Share Knowledge and Resources

The most impactful collaborations are built on mutual benefit. Sharing knowledge, expertise, and resources strengthens the entire network.

For instance, if you're knowledgeable about financial planning, share insights with others looking to improve their financial literacy. Or, if you excel in using a specific software program, mentor colleagues unfamiliar with it. These exchanges build trust and create opportunities for collective growth.

2. Cross-Promote and Support Each Other's Ventures

Collaboration amplifies visibility and reach. When you promote each other's projects, businesses, or initiatives, you create a ripple effect, expanding your collective audience.

This could include sharing content on social media, recommending services to potential clients, or co-hosting events or workshops. Supporting each other's ventures ensures everyone benefits from greater exposure and shared success.

3.Offer Mentorship and Support

One of the most transformative aspects of collaboration is learning from each other's experiences. By mentoring and supporting others, you create a safe space for growth and development.

Think of women in your network who could benefit from your guidance. Share your expertise, provide encouragement, and offer practical advice to help them navigate their careers and personal goals.

4.Advocate for Each Other's Success

Be a champion for the women in your network. Celebrate their accomplishments, support their promotions, and speak up for them when they face challenges.

Advocacy fosters a culture of solidarity and reinforces a shared commitment to success. By amplifying each other's voices, you demonstrate your belief in their potential and create an environment where everyone can thrive.

5. Create Inclusive Spaces

Inclusivity is the foundation of successful collaboration. It ensures that everyone feels valued, respected, and heard.

This means actively listening to diverse perspectives, acknowledging different backgrounds, and fostering an environment where everyone can contribute their unique talents and insights.

WHY COLLABORATION MATTERS

Cultivating a collaborative environment requires consistent effort and a shift in mindset. It's about replacing the "me vs. them" mentality with the power of "we." By prioritizing collaboration over competition, women of color can become a driving force for positive change—not just for themselves but for future generations.

REAL-LIFE EXAMPLES OF COLLABORATION
Collaboration as a Source of Innovation

Renowned architect Zaha Hadid revolutionized the field of architecture with her visionary designs. However, her success was not achieved in isolation. She consistently collaborated with a team of architects, engineers, and artists, fostering an environment where ideas were challenged and refined.

This collaborative approach led to groundbreaking designs that redefined architectural norms, showcasing how teamwork can inspire innovation and produce extraordinary results.

Collaboration as a Force for Equity

The MeToo movement exemplifies the power of collective action. Women from diverse backgrounds shared their stories of harassment and abuse, creating a unified call for accountability and justice.

This movement demonstrated how collaboration amplifies voices, challenges entrenched power structures, and sparks meaningful change on a global scale.

Collaboration as a Pathway to Economic Empowerment

The rise of Black-owned businesses in recent years highlights the strength of community collaboration. Black entrepreneurs have increasingly shared resources, marketing expertise, and financial support to build a thriving ecosystem.

These partnerships have fostered economic empowerment, creating opportunities for businesses to grow and contributing to the prosperity of the Black community.

Embracing a Culture of Collaboration

Collaboration goes beyond working together on projects. It's about fostering a culture of trust, mutual support, and shared purpose. It's about creating an environment where everyone feels empowered to contribute their unique skills and perspectives.

By embracing this approach, women of color can unlock their collective potential, create lasting opportunities, and shape a more equitable and prosperous future for all.

ALLYSHIP AND ADVOCACY

Allyship goes beyond expressing support—it's about taking meaningful action to dismantle systems of oppression and create environments where everyone feels valued and respected. It's recognizing that each of us has a role in making the world more equitable and inclusive.

Think of allyship as being an active teammate rather than a passive observer. Instead of standing on sidelines, you're contributing to the team's success. In the context of diversity and inclusion, allyship means using your influence and resources to amplify the voices of marginalized groups and challenge discriminatory practices.

Allyship involves advocacy, both for yourself and others. This requires speaking up against injustice, whether it's addressing a microaggression in a meeting or tackling systemic issues that affect entire communities. Advocacy takes courage, but it's essential for driving meaningful change.

PRINCIPLES OF EFFECTIVE ALLYSHIP

1. Educate Yourself

Before you can effectively support others, it's important to understand the issues they face. This means actively seeking out knowledge about the experiences of marginalized groups and exploring the historical roots of inequality.

Engage with diverse perspectives by reading books, articles, and blogs authored by individuals from underrepresented communities. Listen to podcasts and watch documentaries that highlight their stories. True allyship begins with informed understanding.

2. Listen and Believe

When someone shares their experiences with you, listen with intention and empathy. Resist the urge to minimize their experiences or offer unsolicited solutions. Instead, validate their feelings and offer support. Believing their account, even if it challenges your worldview, is a critical step in building trust.

3. Speak Up

Silence can perpetuate harm. When you encounter injustice, speak out. Challenge discriminatory language, biased jokes, and stereotypes. While it's important to be respectful, you should also be firm in addressing harmful behavior.

4. Support Minority-Owned Businesses and Organizations

Where you spend your money matters. By supporting minority-owned businesses and organizations, you contribute to economic empowerment and help create a more equitable society.

5. Advocate for Change

Use your voice and influence to promote policies and practices that foster equality and inclusion. This could mean writing to elected officials, participating in community advocacy, or addressing inequalities in your workplace or personal circles.

6. Recognize Your Privilege

Understanding your privilege is key to effective allyship. Acknowledge how your experiences may differ from those of marginalized groups and use your privilege to create opportunities for others.

7. Be Patient and Persistent

Creating a more equitable world is a marathon, not a sprint. Don't be discouraged by slow progress or setbacks. Consistency and commitment are essential to making a lasting impact.

ALLYSHIP IN ACTION

IN THE WORKPLACE

- **Address Microaggressions:** When a coworker makes an offensive joke or comment, address it directly. Explain why the behavior is harmful and encourage respectful communication in the workplace.
- **Mentor and Sponsor:** Provide guidance to colleagues from underrepresented groups. Help them navigate workplace dynamics, build confidence, and connect with growth opportunities.
- **Promote Diversity in Hiring:** Advocate for fair hiring practices by addressing unconscious biases and ensuring diverse candidates are given equal opportunities.

- **Champion Inclusive Language:** Use language that acknowledges and respects everyone's identities, such as gender-neutral terms in workplace communications.
- **Support Employee Resource Groups (ERGs):** Participate in and advocate for ERGs that focus on addressing the needs and concerns of marginalized employees.

IN THE COMMUNITY

- **Support Local Organizations:** Contribute to organizations that work toward addressing social injustices and uplifting marginalized communities through donations or volunteer work.
- **Speak Against Discrimination:** If you witness discriminatory behavior in your community, address it directly or report it to the appropriate authorities.
- **Educate Family and Friends:** Engage your personal network in conversations about diversity, equity, and inclusion. Help expand their understanding of these important issues.

IN PERSONAL LIFE
- **Challenge Your Own Biases:** Take time to reflect on your assumptions and how they influence your interactions with others. Commit to personal growth in this area.
- **Be an Active Listener:** When friends or family members share their experiences, listen attentively, validate their feelings, and offer support.
- **Celebrate Diversity:** Broaden your perspective by exploring and embracing diverse cultures. Attend cultural events, learn about different traditions, and engage meaningfully with people from various backgrounds.

ALLYSHIP: A LIFELONG JOURNEY

Allyship isn't a one-time action but a continuous journey of learning, growth, and active contribution. By embedding allyship into our daily routines, we help create a world that is inclusive, equitable, and just for everyone.

LEVERAGING SOCIAL CAPITAL

The world of work is built on relationships, connections, and networks. These interactions form your social capital, a valuable resource that can propel you forward in your career.

Social capital isn't just about knowing people; it's about using those connections strategically to unlock opportunities, gain insights, and achieve your goals.

Imagine standing at a bustling conference, surrounded by industry leaders and potential allies. You've prepared your elevator pitch, but how do you navigate the room and make meaningful connections beyond a simple handshake? Understanding the power of social capital and using it intentionally is the key.

Your social capital thrives on proactive networking and authentic relationship-building. Think of your network as a garden that needs care, growth, and diversity. It's your reservoir of advice, inspiration, and support—a treasure chest of opportunities waiting to be unlocked.

BUILDING AND EXPANDING YOUR NETWORK

1. Recognize the Value of Your Existing Connections

You may already belong to various communities, such as alumni associations, professional organizations, or online forums. These groups provide fertile ground for building stronger relationships by attending events, joining committees, or participating in discussions.

Your personal network is equally valuable. Friends, family, mentors, and former colleagues can offer support, advice, and introductions that might advance your career. Remember, your network extends beyond your immediate professional circle.

2. Actively Engage in Networking

Networking is an ongoing process. It involves intentionally seeking new connections, maintaining relationships with like-minded individuals, and staying engaged with your existing network. Attend industry events, participate in webinars, and join relevant online groups to expand your reach.

Networking is not about collecting business cards—it's about building genuine connections. Show sincere interest in others, ask thoughtful questions, and offer support whenever possible. Be a resource for your network by sharing expertise, insights, and even job leads when appropriate.

LEVERAGING ONLINE PLATFORMS

Social media platforms are powerful tools for nurturing your network. Use LinkedIn to connect with professionals, participate in discussions, and share your expertise. Platforms like Twitter can help you engage in industry conversations and connect with thought leaders.

As you grow your network, strive for diversity and inclusivity. Connect with individuals from different industries, backgrounds, and levels of experience. A diverse network broadens your perspective, introduces you to new ideas, and offers invaluable insights.

MENTORSHIP AND SPONSORSHIP

Mentorship and sponsorship are integral to leveraging social capital. A mentor can provide guidance, advice, and support as you navigate your career, while a sponsor can champion your achievements and open doors to new opportunities.

Finally, remember that social capital works both ways. Be a dependable and supportive member of your network—offer help when it's needed and celebrate the achievements of others. By embracing a spirit of mutual support and cooperation, you can build a network that is genuinely meaningful, rewarding, and empowering.

Let's look at real-life examples to understand the impact of utilizing social capital effectively.

SOCIAL CAPITAL IN ACTION

Scenario 1: Transitioning to a New Industry

You're looking to change industries. A friend in that field shares insights about potential employers, key skills, and industry trends, helping you make a smooth transition.

Scenario 2: Preparing for a Job Interview

You reach out to a mentor with extensive interview experience. Their advice and guidance give you the confidence to excel in your upcoming interview.

Scenario 3: Pursuing a Leadership Role

You lack leadership experience but connect with a seasoned leader in your network. Their mentorship equips you with the skills and confidence to succeed in a leadership position.

These examples illustrate the tangible benefits of leveraging social capital to unlock opportunities, gain insights, and achieve your career goals.

However, it's important to remember that social capital is not a quick path to success. It is a resource that requires thoughtful development, consistent effort, and authentic relationships. Building social capital means forming meaningful connections, sharing your knowledge, and contributing to the success of others. By focusing on genuine interactions, you can harness the full potential of your social capital and build a network that supports your growth and success in your professional journey.

EXPANDING SOCIAL CAPITAL: BEYOND NETWORKING

While networking is a vital aspect of leveraging your social capital, it's essential to broaden your perspective and explore other avenues to strengthen your connections.

1. Community Engagement

Participate in volunteer work, join local organizations, or attend community events to build relationships with individuals from diverse backgrounds. This broadens your perspective and enhances your empathy.

2. Online Platforms and Social Media

In addition to LinkedIn explore platforms aligned with your industry or interests. Engage in online communities and forums to foster meaningful connections.

3. Mentorship and Sponsorship Programs

Seek mentorship opportunities and offer guidance to others. Sharing your expertise can empower the next generation of professionals.

4. Professional Associations and Industry Groups

Get involved in associations relevant to your field. Attend events, join committees, and contribute to discussions to expand your network.

5. Cultivating Collaboration

Encourage teamwork, open communication, and mutual support in your workplace. A collaborative environment creates opportunities for growth and success.

6. Building Trust and Reciprocity

Strong relationships thrive on trust and mutual support. Be reliable, offer help, and celebrate the successes of others in your network.

USING SOCIAL CAPITAL FOR GREATER IMPACT

1. Advocate for Inclusivity and Diversity

Use your network to promote inclusivity and diversity. Raise awareness of the unique challenges faced by minority women and champion equal opportunities.

2. Support Women-Owned Businesses

Promote entrepreneurship by supporting women-owned businesses. Share their stories, recommend their products or services, and collaborate when possible.

3. Mentor the Next Generation

Empower young women by mentoring and guiding them to pursue their goals and dreams.

4. Create a Legacy of Change

Leverage your social capital to contribute to a more equitable and inclusive world, leaving a legacy of positive change.

THE POWER OF SOCIAL CAPITAL

Social capital is a tool that, when nurtured with intention, unlocks opportunities, accelerates careers, and creates lasting impact. By building genuine connections, advocating for inclusivity, and collaborating effectively, you can create a network that empowers you to thrive in your professional journey.

CULTIVATING SUPPORTIVE COMMUNITIES

Think about the powerful network of women you admire—your mentors, your friends, your colleagues. Each one contributes to your support system, offering unique perspectives and experiences. These connections provide invaluable guidance, encouragement, and a sense of belonging, especially when navigating the unique challenges minority women face in the professional world.

Building a community that uplifts and empowers you is not just about attending networking events or joining online groups. It's about forming genuine connections with people who share your values, understand your challenges, and are ready to offer a listening ear or a helping hand. These communities create safe spaces where you can share triumphs, celebrate wins, and work through setbacks together.

Imagine a group of women gathered around a table, each sharing stories of overcoming obstacles, strategies for navigating workplace dynamics, and insights on balancing personal and professional responsibilities. In such a setting, you are not just a participant—you are part of a collective, drawing strength from shared experiences and celebrating each other's progress.

FINDING YOUR TRIBE

- **Start with your existing network:** Look beyond your immediate circle. Reach out to women in your industry, community, or those who share a passion for a specific cause.
- **Attend industry events:** Participate in conferences, workshops, and meetups related to your field or interests. These gatherings provide opportunities to connect with like-minded individuals.

- **Join professional organizations:** Look for organizations that support minority women or promote diversity and inclusion. These groups often offer mentorship, networking opportunities, and valuable resources.
- **Volunteer:** Get involved in causes that align with your values. Volunteering often leads to unexpected connections with individuals who share your passions.
- **Explore online communities:** Join forums, social media groups, and digital spaces dedicated to empowering minority women. Engage in discussions, share your experiences, and offer support to others.

CULTIVATING DEEP CONNECTIONS

- **Engage in meaningful conversations:** Move beyond surface-level interactions by asking open-ended questions that encourage genuine dialogue and shared insights.
- **Offer support and mentorship:** Be a source of encouragement and guidance for others by sharing your knowledge and experiences.

- **Embrace vulnerability:** Share your struggles and challenges. This builds trust and fosters authentic relationships.
- **Celebrate successes:** Acknowledge and cheer on each other's achievements, creating a positive and uplifting environment.
- **Respect differences:** Welcome diverse perspectives and experiences within your community.

NURTURING A SUPPORTIVE COMMUNITY

- **Host events and gatherings:** Organize social events, workshops, or mentorship programs to strengthen bonds within your network.
- **Create a shared vision:** Develop a common goal or purpose that unites your community and fosters collaboration.
- **Promote inclusivity:** Ensure your community is welcoming to women from all backgrounds and experiences.
- **Maintain open communication:** Encourage open dialogue and constructive feedback to address concerns effectively.

- **Celebrate milestones:** Mark important milestones to strengthen the sense of shared progress and achievement.

THE STRENGTH OF COLLECTIVE SUPPORT

Creating a supportive community isn't just about networking—it's about cultivating a space where you feel seen, heard, and valued. It's about surrounding yourself with women who inspire, challenge, and lift you higher.

Imagine a group of women in a boardroom, each a leader in her field, sharing insights and strategies for breaking barriers and paving the way for future generations. This shared determination creates a ripple effect that goes beyond individual achievements. It's a testament to the power of community, where mutual support becomes the foundation for meaningful change.

NAVIGATING CHALLENGES

Building a supportive community isn't always easy. Differences in opinions, personalities, or experiences can lead to challenges. Addressing conflicts with respect, engaging in constructive dialogue, and seeking common ground are essential.

Remember, community building is a journey, not a destination. It requires continuous effort, honest communication, and a commitment to mutual support. When you encounter obstacles, lean on your community for guidance, encouragement, and renewed motivation.

A NETWORK OF INSPIRATION

Think of your community as a source of inspiration. Each woman brings her own story, skills, and perspective. This diversity creates a rich pool of wisdom, encouragement, and support.

Picture a young woman navigating the challenges of a male-dominated industry. She connects with a mentor in her community—a professional who understands her struggles. This mentor shares valuable advice and provides a sense of belonging, helping the young woman navigate her career with confidence.

This mentoring relationship, formed within a supportive community, inspires not only the mentee but others who witness its impact. The ripple effect motivates even more women to pursue their goals and lift others along the way.

A CATALYST FOR CHANGE

Building supportive communities goes beyond personal growth—it becomes a catalyst for transformation. By working together, minority women can advocate for greater inclusivity and equity in society.

Consider the countless women who paved the way for those who followed. From activists fighting for equal rights to trailblazers breaking barriers in corporate spaces, their collective efforts have carved a path for future generations.

By fostering communities that empower minority women, we continue this legacy, ensuring every woman has the opportunity to thrive, lead, and create meaningful change in the world.

CHAPTER 5

BALANCING PERSONAL AND PROFESSIONAL LIFE

TIME MANAGEMENT TECHNIQUES

The constant push-and-pull between professional and personal responsibilities can feel overwhelming. Minority women, in particular, often contend with societal expectations, workplace biases, and family duties, creating a unique juggling act. This chapter offers practical strategies to help you navigate these challenges and design a life that thrives in all aspects.

The cornerstone of achieving balance lies in effective time management. Time is one of our most valuable resources, and how we choose to spend it directly impacts our success, happiness, and well-being. Imagine your time as a limited budget. Each minute you use is an investment, and prioritizing wisely allows you to maximize returns in both your professional and personal life.

THE ART OF PRIORITIZATION

Start by reflecting on how you currently spend your time. Are your days filled with tasks that truly matter, or are they consumed by less impactful activities? Honest self-assessment is key to identifying where adjustments can be made.

Next, organize your tasks by urgency and importance using the Eisenhower Matrix, a proven time management tool:

- **Urgent and Important:** Handle these tasks immediately—they are your top priority.
- **Important but Not Urgent:** Plan and schedule these tasks; they are essential for long-term success.
- **Urgent but Not Important:** These are distractions that can be delegated or minimized.
- **Not Urgent and Not Important:** Avoid these time-wasters whenever possible.

By focusing on the first two categories, you can channel your energy toward meaningful, high-impact activities while reducing the stress of constant demands.

TIME-BLOCKING: A PRACTICAL STRATEGY FOR PRODUCTIVITY

Once you've prioritized your tasks, implement a time-blocking system. Time-blocking assigns specific time slots to activities, creating structure and reducing distractions.

For example, instead of attempting to complete a project in one undefined stretch of time, break it into smaller steps. Dedicate an hour to research, another hour to writing, and a third to editing. This method promotes focus and clarity, ensuring you're giving your best to each task.

LEVERAGING TECHNOLOGY TO STAY ORGANIZED

In the digital age, there are countless tools available to enhance productivity and time management. Explore task management apps like Trello, Asana, or Todoist to create lists, set deadlines, and track progress. These apps keep your priorities visible and manageable.

Scheduling tools like Google Calendar are invaluable for keeping track of appointments, meetings, and personal commitments. Use them to avoid scheduling conflicts and to receive reminders, ensuring nothing slips through the cracks.

SETTING BOUNDARIES: PROTECTING YOUR TIME AND ENERGY

Time management isn't about cramming more into your day—it's about creating a sustainable rhythm that supports your overall well-being. Setting boundaries is a critical part of this process.

Boundaries help you safeguard your time and energy. They might include:

- Saying "no" to commitments that don't align with your goals.
- Delegating tasks when possible.
- Taking regular breaks to recharge.
- Establishing specific work hours and sticking to them.

These practices ensure you have the capacity for personal growth, family, and self-care.

THE POWER OF PLANNING

Planning isn't just about making a to-do list—it's about aligning your daily activities with your broader goals. Take time each week to map out your schedule. Include professional responsibilities, personal commitments, and time for self-care. By being intentional, you can actively shape your life instead of reacting to it.

MINDFUL TIME MANAGEMENT

True time management involves more than following a strict schedule; it requires mindfulness. Stay present in the moment, focus on one task at a time, and resist the temptation to multitask. Make conscious choices about your activities, prioritizing those that enhance your well-being and align with your goals.

THE IMPORTANCE OF SELF-CARE

Time management isn't solely about productivity—it's also about making space for self-care. Prioritizing activities that nurture your physical, mental, and emotional well-being is essential for a balanced life. This could include regular exercise, mindfulness practices, hobbies, or spending time with loved ones.

Make self-care a non-negotiable part of your routine. Treat it with the same importance as a major work project or family obligation. Self-care isn't indulgent; it's foundational to your long-term health and happiness.

BUILDING A STRONG SUPPORT SYSTEM

Balancing life's demands can feel overwhelming, but you don't have to face it alone. Cultivate a support system of friends, family, mentors, and colleagues. These connections offer emotional support, practical help, and a sense of belonging, reducing stress and feelings of isolation.

CONCLUSION

Mastering time management is a journey that involves continual refinement. You will encounter obstacles, but by applying these strategies, you can create a life that feels balanced and fulfilling.

Remember, the goal isn't to fit everything into your schedule—it's to design a life that reflects your values and aspirations. By prioritizing your well-being, setting boundaries, and embracing a mindful approach to time, you can take control of your life and create a meaningful, sustainable future.

SETTING PRIORITIES AND GOALS

Imagine you're a chef preparing a gourmet meal. You have a variety of ingredients, each with unique qualities. Success doesn't come from throwing everything into the pot at once—it requires careful planning, prioritization, and balance. Similarly, managing your time and achieving your goals, especially while balancing personal and professional life, requires intentionality and strategy.

Just as a chef follows a structured recipe, you need a clear plan for managing your time and energy. This plan involves identifying your priorities, setting realistic goals, and using your resources effectively.

Think of your priorities as the foundation of your life. They represent what matters most—nurturing your family, advancing your career, or dedicating time to your passions. Once you understand your priorities, you can pursue your goals with clarity and focus.

PRACTICAL STRATEGIES FOR SETTING PRIORITIES AND GOALS

1. Reflect and Define

Take a moment to reflect on your values and aspirations. What truly matters to you? What brings joy, fulfillment, and purpose? Write down your core values and long-term dreams to clarify your non-negotiables and the life you envision.

2. Identify Your "Big Rocks"

Imagine filling a jar with sand and small pebbles. If you add these first, there's no room for larger rocks. But if you place the big rocks—your priorities—in first, the smaller items can fit around them. Focus on your "big rocks" to ensure your most important goals take precedence over less critical tasks.

3. Use Time-Blocking

Time-blocking is a practical tool for structuring your day. Assign specific time slots for high-priority activities like brainstorming career strategies, spending time with loved ones, or exercising. Scheduling tasks in advance ensures focus and productivity.

4. Set SMART Goals

Create SMART goals that are:

- **Specific:** Clearly define what you aim to achieve.
- **Measurable:** Set criteria to track progress.
- **Achievable:** Ensure your goal is realistic.
- **Relevant:** Align your goals with your priorities and values.
- **Time-bound:** Assign a deadline to maintain momentum and accountability.

5. Embrace Delegation

Delegating tasks is not about offloading responsibilities but working strategically to free your time for higher-impact activities. Trust others with tasks that don't require your direct attention to maximize efficiency and foster collaboration.

6. Apply the 80/20 Rule

The Pareto Principle suggests that 80% of your outcomes come from 20% of your efforts. Focus on the critical few tasks that create the most significant results. Let go of or simplify tasks with minimal impact.

7. Practice Flexibility

Life is unpredictable. Be ready to adjust your plans and goals based on new circumstances or opportunities. Regularly re-evaluate your priorities to ensure they align with your current situation.

8. Learn to Say No

Politely declining tasks or commitments that don't align with your priorities protects your time and energy. Saying "no" allows you to focus on what truly matters.

9. Visualize Your Goals

Use visual tools like planners, whiteboards, or apps to organize and track your progress. A clear visual representation keeps your priorities top of mind and motivates you to stay on track.

10. Celebrate Milestones

Break large goals into smaller, manageable milestones. Celebrate each accomplishment to maintain motivation and recognize your progress.

SHIFTING FROM "TO-DO" TO "TO-BE"

Setting priorities and goals isn't just about organizing tasks—it's about shaping a life that reflects your values and aspirations. By focusing on your "big rocks" and allocating your time and energy purposefully, you move beyond a simple to-do list to creating a life centered on who you want to be.

Think of it as a well-designed puzzle, where each piece plays a vital role in creating a complete and meaningful picture. By intentionally choosing how to invest your time and energy, you can build a life that is both rewarding and purposeful.

Real-Life Examples of Prioritization

Mia's Story

Mia, a single mother and marketing manager, struggled to balance her career and family life. She identified spending quality time with her daughter as a non-negotiable priority. By using time-blocking, she scheduled regular family dinners and playtime, adjusting her work schedule and delegating tasks as needed. She also set a SMART goal to save for a family vacation, ensuring meaningful time with her daughter.

Mark's Approach

Mark, an entrepreneur, faced burnout from trying to manage every aspect of his business. Applying the 80/20 Rule, he identified high-impact tasks and delegated others to his team. This allowed him to focus on long-term strategies and personal growth, rediscovering balance and energy.

THE IMPORTANCE OF FLEXIBILITY

Life's unpredictability can require sudden changes to plans. Flexibility is essential for maintaining balance and responding to unexpected challenges. Periodically revisit your priorities to ensure they reflect your evolving needs and opportunities.

BUILDING A LIFE OF PURPOSE

Prioritizing and setting achievable goals creates a foundation for a life of purpose and fulfillment. By consciously aligning your actions with your values, you move beyond time management to intentionally designing your life. This ongoing journey requires reflection, adaptation, and a commitment to growth, but it empowers you to live authentically and with intention.

SELF-CARE AND WELLBEING

Imagine yourself as a vibrant flower blooming in a field of equally beautiful blossoms. Just as a flower needs sunlight, water, and nourishing soil to grow, you, as a minority woman, require self-care to thrive in both your personal and professional life. This chapter explores the essential practice of self-care, highlighting its ability to sustain your well-being and help you navigate the complexities of life.

Self-care isn't about indulging in occasional luxuries like spa days or fancy meals. It's a comprehensive approach to meeting your physical, mental, emotional, and spiritual needs. It involves recognizing your limits, respecting your boundaries, and prioritizing your health and happiness. Think of self-care as an investment in yourself—one that yields resilience, productivity, and long-term fulfillment.

Let's begin by understanding that self-care isn't a luxury; it's a necessity. Just as a car requires regular maintenance to function optimally, you must prioritize self-care to keep yourself energized and balanced. The demands of navigating a world that often overlooks you, combined with work deadlines, household responsibilities, and social pressures, can take a toll on your overall well-being.

Neglecting self-care can lead to burnout, heightened stress, anxiety, and even depression. It drains your energy, strains relationships, and diminishes your capacity to perform effectively. In a world that expects constant strength and adaptability, neglecting self-care leaves you feeling depleted and overwhelmed.

BUILDING A PERSONAL SELF-CARE RITUAL

Self-care is about making conscious choices to nurture your body, mind, and soul. Here are ways to create a routine tailored to your needs:

- **Mindful Movement:** Engage in physical activities you enjoy, such as yoga, dancing, swimming, or hiking. Movement releases endorphins, reduces stress, and boosts your mood.
- **Nurturing Your Mind:** Dedicate time to activities that stimulate your mind, such as reading, writing, learning a new skill, or exploring creative pursuits. These keep you engaged, reduce stress, and enhance cognitive function.
- **Prioritizing Sleep:** Quality sleep is vital for restoring your energy. Aim for 7–9 hours nightly by creating a calming bedtime routine, limiting screen time, and optimizing your sleep environment.
- **Connecting with Nature:** Spending time outdoors improves well-being. Walk in the park, garden, or simply sit under a tree to recharge.
- **Nourishing Your Body:** Fuel yourself with nutritious meals featuring whole foods, fruits,

vegetables, and lean proteins to sustain energy and overall health.

- **Unplugging from Technology:** Limit screen time to reduce stress and improve focus. Set clear boundaries for when you're "off-duty" from devices.
- **Practicing Mindfulness and Meditation:** Incorporate mindfulness or meditation into your routine to cultivate calmness, reduce stress, and enhance self-awareness.
- **Connecting with Loved Ones:** Strengthen relationships by spending time with supportive friends and family who provide emotional connection and a sense of belonging.
- **Setting Boundaries:** Learn to say "no" to draining requests. Prioritize your needs and limit how others access your time and energy.
- **Seeking Professional Support:** If you're experiencing stress or mental health concerns, seek help from a therapist or counselor for guidance and coping strategies.

Remember, self-care isn't selfish; it's self-preservation. By taking care of yourself, you become better equipped to face challenges, nurture relationships, and excel in your career.

SELF-CARE AS A CATALYST FOR GROWTH AND RESILIENCE

Here's how self-care empowers you to navigate life's challenges:

- **Building Resilience:** Regular self-care enhances your ability to recover from setbacks and approach challenges with confidence.
- **Fostering Emotional Intelligence:** Nurturing your mental and emotional health helps you manage your emotions and respond thoughtfully to others.
- **Improving Communication:** A clear and calm mind improves communication, strengthening personal and professional relationships.
- **Boosting Productivity:** Prioritizing self-care energizes you, improving focus and efficiency, which leads to better outcomes.
- **Increasing Confidence:** Taking care of yourself builds self-esteem, enabling you to advocate for your needs and take on leadership roles.

Self-care isn't an occasional indulgence—it's a daily commitment. Consider integrating small, impactful practices into your day, such as starting the morning with mindfulness, enjoying a healthy breakfast, or taking a short walk. Throughout the day, take breaks to recharge, listen to music, or stretch. In the evening, unwind with a relaxing activity like reading, journaling, or a warm bath.

SELF-CARE: A PATHWAY TO EMPOWERMENT

As a minority woman navigating life's unique challenges, self-care is an essential tool for overcoming obstacles, building resilience, and creating a meaningful life. It's a reminder that you are not just a role—employee, mother, sister, or friend—you are a complete individual deserving of care and attention.

By prioritizing self-care, you enable yourself to approach life with strength, grace, and clarity. The benefits extend beyond you, impacting your workplace, relationships, and community.

FINDING SUPPORT AND BUILDING COMMUNITY

You're not alone on this journey. Surround yourself with a network of supportive individuals who understand your experiences. Join groups, connect with mentors, and celebrate shared achievements. A strong sense of community fosters emotional support, guidance, and a sense of belonging.

Investing in your well-being isn't just about you—it's a foundation for achieving success in all areas of your life. By embracing self-care, you take a stand for yourself, creating a life that reflects your values and aspirations.

MANAGING STRESS AND BURNOUT

We've all felt it—that mounting pressure, the endless to-do list, and the constant feeling of being on edge. Stress is a silent yet powerful force that can erode well-being over time. For minority women balancing the complexities of professional and personal life, stress can be especially impactful.

Burnout, an advanced state of chronic stress, is a serious concern. It manifests as emotional, physical, and mental exhaustion, often accompanied by feelings of cynicism, detachment, and diminished effectiveness. Burnout isn't just about being overwhelmed; it's about feeling deeply depleted and unable to cope.

Recognizing the warning signs of burnout is crucial. Here are some indicators:

- **Physical Exhaustion:** Persistent fatigue, even after rest, along with body aches, frequent headaches, or difficulty managing simple tasks.
- **Emotional Depletion:** Feelings of numbness, detachment, or cynicism. Activities that once brought joy now feel uninspiring.
- **Mental Fogginess:** Difficulty concentrating, making decisions, or remembering things. Tasks may feel insurmountable.
- **Increased Irritability:** Frustration, impatience, or anger directed at colleagues, family, or even yourself.
- **Sleep Disturbances:** Trouble falling or staying asleep, or waking up feeling unrefreshed.
- **Physical Symptoms:** Unexplained aches, digestive issues, or changes in appetite.

If these signs resonate with you, it's time to take proactive steps. Ignoring burnout can lead to a vicious cycle of worsening stress, reduced productivity, and potential health problems.

STRATEGIES FOR MANAGING STRESS AND AVOIDING BURNOUT

1. Prioritize Self-Care

Self-care is essential for maintaining your physical, mental, and emotional health. Tailor it to your unique needs:

- **Physical Health:** Prioritize adequate sleep, nutritious meals, and regular physical activity. Exercise, even in small amounts, can relieve stress and improve your mood.
- **Mental Wellness:** Practice mindfulness, meditation, or relaxation techniques. Dedicate time to activities that bring you joy, such as reading, listening to music, or spending time outdoors.
- **Emotional Support:** Share your challenges with a trusted friend, family member, or therapist. Talking through your feelings can provide relief and perspective.

2. Set Realistic Expectations

Perfectionism often fuels stress. Learn to embrace imperfection and focus on what truly matters:

- **Identify Priorities:** Clarify what's most important and channel your energy into those areas.

- **Break Down Tasks:** Divide large projects into smaller, manageable steps to make them less daunting.
- **Schedule Breaks:** Incorporate short breaks into your day to recharge and refocus.

3. Manage Your Time Effectively

Time management isn't about doing more—it's about doing what matters most:

- **Create a Schedule:** Plan your day to balance work and personal responsibilities.
- **Use Time Blocking:** Assign specific time slots for tasks to improve focus and efficiency.
- **Delegate Tasks:** Handoff responsibilities where possible to free up your time and energy for higher-priority activities.

4. Cultivate Healthy Boundaries

Maintaining clear boundaries between work and personal life is key to reducing stress:

- **Define Your Limits:** Communicate your work hours and availability to colleagues and clients.
- **Limit Screen Time:** Especially in the evenings, disconnect from devices to unwind.
- **Prioritize Quality Time:** Dedicate time to activities that bring joy and nourish your soul.

5. Build a Supportive Network

A strong network of positive relationships can be a powerful stress reliever:

- **Seek Mentors:** Connect with individuals who can offer guidance and support.
- **Join Communities:** Engage with groups of like-minded women for shared experiences and encouragement.
- **Strengthen Relationships:** Invest in personal connections with family and friends to foster emotional well-being.

6. Seek Professional Help

When stress becomes overwhelming, professional assistance can be invaluable:

- **Therapy:** A therapist can help you develop strategies for managing stress and improving overall mental health.
- **Counseling:** A counselor can work with you to address underlying issues contributing to stress.
- **Support Groups:** Joining a group can provide a sense of community and shared understanding.

CREATING A BALANCED LIFE

Managing stress and preventing burnout isn't about heroic efforts or neglecting your needs. It's about intentional actions that prioritize your physical, mental, and emotional health.

By embracing self-care, setting realistic expectations, improving time management, establishing boundaries, building a supportive network, and seeking professional help when needed, you can create a balanced and fulfilling life—both professionally and personally.

CREATING A SUPPORT SYSTEM

The journey toward balancing your professional and personal life is ongoing, requiring mindfulness and a robust support system. Building this system isn't just about having people around; it's about cultivating meaningful connections that provide the emotional, practical, and intellectual resources you need to thrive.

Imagine this: You're at a crossroads, faced with a major career decision. Work deadlines loom, family commitments pile up, and a personal project ignites your passion. For many women—particularly minority women navigating systemic barriers and cultural expectations—this scenario is all too familiar. The pressure can be overwhelming, leading to feelings of anxiety and even burnout. But what if you had a network of people who truly understood your challenges, offered sound advice, and provided a listening ear? That's the power of a supportive system.

CULTIVATING YOUR CIRCLE OF SUPPORT

Think of your support system as a toolkit filled with individuals who bring diverse strengths and perspectives. This "toolkit" might include:

- **Mentors:** Experienced individuals who guide you based on their own journeys. Mentors offer insights, share lessons learned, and provide constructive feedback. They may come from your professional network, organizations, or even your family.
- **Sponsors:** Advocates who actively promote your career advancement by opening doors to opportunities and championing your talents. Unlike mentors, sponsors take an active role in endorsing your potential.
- **Accountability Partners:** Friends, colleagues, or family members who motivate you, check on your progress, and encourage you to stay focused on

your goals. They help you overcome procrastination and self-doubt.

- **Close Friends and Family:** Your immediate circle serves as emotional anchors, offering unconditional support, a listening ear, and shared celebrations of your successes.
- **Professional Networks:** Engaging with professional groups, attending conferences, and joining industry-specific organizations provides valuable insights, opportunities, and connections.
- **Therapists or Counselors:** Professional guidance from therapists or counselors can help you manage stress, navigate personal challenges, and maintain a healthy work-life balance.

NURTURING AND EXPANDING YOUR SUPPORT SYSTEM

Building a strong support network is an ongoing effort. Here's how to expand and strengthen it:

- **Be Intentional:** Build relationships by engaging in genuine conversations, actively listening, and offering support in return.

- **Attend Industry Events:** Conferences, workshops, and networking events provide opportunities to meet like-minded individuals and expand your professional circle.
- **Seek Mentorship:** Identify individuals you admire and reach out for guidance. Express your interest in learning from their experiences.
- **Mentor Others:** Offer your knowledge and support to others. Mentorship not only benefits the mentee but also enhances your leadership skills and broadens your network.
- **Collaborate:** Work on joint projects or initiatives with colleagues or peers. Collaboration builds trust and shared achievements.
- **Volunteer:** Contribute your time and expertise to causes that align with your values. This allows you to connect with people who share your passions.
- **Embrace Technology:** Use social media platforms and professional networking sites to connect with individuals in your field and stay informed about opportunities.

THE IMPORTANCE OF DIVERSITY IN YOUR SUPPORT SYSTEM

Diversity enriches your support system by bringing varied perspectives and experiences:

- **Cultural Diversity:** Connecting with individuals from different cultural backgrounds broadens your worldview and challenges your thinking.
- **Professional Diversity:** Interacting with people from various industries or career paths exposes you to fresh ideas and new approaches.
- **Generational Diversity:** Relationships with individuals from different age groups provide insights into historical contexts, emerging trends, and growth strategies.

CREATING A SUPPORTIVE ENVIRONMENT FOR OTHERS

As you build your network, remember to support others as well:

- **Offer Mentorship:** Share your experiences and knowledge to help others navigate their journeys.
- **Advocate for Inclusion:** Promote diversity and inclusivity in your workplace and community.

- **Foster Collaboration:** Encourage teamwork, open communication, and mutual support within your network.

NAVIGATING CHALLENGES IN BUILDING SUPPORT

Building and maintaining a support system isn't without challenges. Here's how to address common obstacles:

- **Set Boundaries:** Clearly communicate your needs and limits to ensure relationships remain respectful and mutually beneficial.
- **Handle Conflict Constructively:** Use empathy, active listening, and conflict resolution skills to navigate disagreements.
- **Manage Difficult Relationships:** If certain individuals drain your energy or fail to support you, establish boundaries or, if necessary, distance yourself.

THE POWER OF A STRONG SUPPORT SYSTEM

A strong support system serves as your guiding light through the complexities of life. It offers strength, guidance, and encouragement, helping you overcome challenges, achieve goals, and maintain your well-being. Cultivating and nurturing this network is a continuous journey, but the rewards are profound.

EMBRACING THE JOURNEY

Building a support system isn't about finding the perfect network overnight. It's about cultivating meaningful relationships that nourish your mind, body, and spirit. By investing in your support system, you're investing in your own growth and resilience, empowering yourself to navigate personal and professional demands with confidence and grace.

CHAPTER 6

ADVOCATING FOR YOURSELF

ARTICULATING YOUR VALUE

Picture yourself in a boardroom, presenting your latest project to a group of senior executives. Your heart pounds as you meticulously explain the details of your plan, showcasing innovative solutions and thorough analysis. But as you navigate through your presentation, a nagging question arises: Are they truly understanding your value? Are they acknowledging your expertise?

For many minority women in the workplace, this scenario is all too familiar. They often face challenges in being heard and recognized for their contributions. The perception of "not being taken seriously" stems from systemic biases that undervalue their skills and achievements. This highlights the critical need for self-advocacy — the ability to confidently articulate your value.

Self-advocacy isn't about being loud or aggressive; it's about effectively communicating your worth in a way that resonates with others. It involves recognizing your strengths, quantifying your accomplishments, and showcasing your impact with clarity and assurance.

A SKILL, NOT A TRAIT

Self-advocacy is a skill that can be learned and refined. It's not about being born with natural charisma or an outgoing personality. Instead, it requires developing strategies to highlight your contributions, engage in meaningful conversations, and express your needs and expectations.

Consider Maya, a young professional who consistently delivers outstanding work but struggles to gain recognition. Despite her reputation for attention to detail and creative problem-solving, she feels overlooked in meetings and hesitates to voice her ideas. Over time, she begins questioning her value and feels her efforts are taken for granted.

This is a common experience for many minority women. They may excel in their roles but lack the confidence to effectively communicate their value. Modesty, fear of being labeled "too aggressive," or past experiences of being dismissed can lead to self-doubt.

THE POWER OF STORYTELLING

Breaking through these barriers often begins with storytelling. Instead of simply listing achievements, craft narratives that highlight your impact and make your contributions memorable.

For example, instead of saying, "I successfully implemented a new software system," you might say, "I implemented a new software system that streamlined workflows by 20%, increasing productivity by 15%." This shift transforms a factual statement into a compelling story that emphasizes tangible results.

Similarly, instead of, "I'm a skilled communicator," try, "I bridged the gap between marketing and sales, leading to a 10% increase in customer acquisition." This approach showcases your skills and their direct impact.

BUILDING YOUR NARRATIVE

To build a compelling narrative, reflect on your experiences and identify moments that illustrate your value. Ask yourself:

- What challenges have you overcome?
- What unique perspectives do you bring?
- How have your contributions impacted your team or organization?
- What are your key skills and strengths?
- What are your achievements, and how can you quantify them?

Maya, for instance, began compiling a portfolio of her projects, highlighting challenges she overcame and their positive outcomes. She also started speaking up in meetings, sharing insights, and proposing solutions.

CONFIDENCE THROUGH PREPARATION

Effective self-advocacy requires preparation and practice. Here are actionable steps:

- **Craft an elevator pitch:** Develop a concise summary of your skills and experiences.
- **Prepare for performance reviews:** Track your achievements throughout the year and present them confidently during reviews.
- **Seek feedback:** Request constructive input from colleagues and mentors to refine your communication style.
- **Join professional networks:** Engage with peers to gain insights and opportunities to practice advocacy skills.

BEYOND THE WORKPLACE

The principles of self-advocacy apply in all aspects of life, from negotiating salaries to advocating for family needs. Knowing how to articulate your value empowers you to navigate life with confidence.

Remember, self-advocacy is an ongoing journey. By continually refining your skills and building confidence, you can achieve your goals and inspire others along the way.

NEGOTIATING FOR WHAT YOU DESERVE

Negotiating for what you deserve is an essential skill for minority women, empowering them to claim their rightful place and value in the workplace. It's not just about salary—it's about securing a career path that aligns with your goals, ensuring fair treatment, and gaining the recognition and opportunities you deserve. While the negotiation process can feel intimidating, particularly when facing potential biases or systemic challenges, the right strategies and a confident mindset can help you overcome obstacles and achieve successful outcomes.

Think of negotiation as a partnership—a balanced exchange where both parties work toward a mutually beneficial agreement. It's not about winning or losing but about finding a resolution that respects your needs while addressing the other party's interests. To succeed, you must first build a solid understanding of your worth. This involves a thorough self-assessment, knowing your market value, and believing in your capabilities.

Start by evaluating your skills, experiences, and achievements. Quantify your accomplishments whenever possible. Bring concrete examples of how you've exceeded expectations, contributed significant value to your organization, or made a measurable impact in your role.

Research your industry and comparable positions to gather insights into salary ranges and career pathways. This preparation equips you to confidently present your worth during negotiations.

Remember, negotiation is not just about asking for more—it's about demonstrating the value you bring. Craft a persuasive case that highlights your contributions, your potential for growth, and the unique skills you offer. Emphasize your strengths, dedication to your work, and readiness to go above and beyond. Be prepared to address potential concerns and propose solutions that align with organizational goals.

Effective negotiation hinges on clear, respectful communication. Practice expressing your needs and expectations assertively but without aggression. Present your perspective as part of a collaborative effort to achieve shared goals. Listen carefully to the other party's concerns, showing empathy and understanding. While compromise is often necessary, never settle for less than you know you deserve.

When negotiating, focus on the long-term benefits. Don't concentrate solely on immediate financial rewards. Consider how your negotiation impacts your career growth and future opportunities. Negotiating for a higher salary sets a stronger foundation for future earnings. Additionally, advocating for flexible work arrangements, professional development, or greater autonomy can significantly enhance your career trajectory and overall satisfaction.

The negotiation process, while challenging, can be an empowering experience. It's an opportunity to advocate for yourself, assert your worth, and take meaningful steps toward building a fulfilling career. For minority women, the ability to negotiate effectively is a powerful tool, breaking down barriers and opening doors to advancement and achievement.

HERE ARE SOME ADDITIONAL TIPS FOR SUCCESSFUL NEGOTIATION:

1. Be Prepared:

Enter negotiations with thorough preparation. Research the company, industry standards, and comparable salaries. Identify your strengths and weaknesses and create a clear list of desired outcomes.

2. Know Your Worth:

Understand the value you bring to the company. Be prepared to articulate your skills, experience, and accomplishments to highlight your contributions effectively.

3. Be Confident:

Confidence is crucial. Believe in your worth and practice your negotiation points to ensure you feel self-assured.

4. Be Assertive:

Clearly state your expectations and stand firm in your position. However, remain open to compromise where necessary.

5. Be Respectful:

Advocate for yourself while respecting the other party. Active listening and mutual respect are key to successful negotiations.

6. Don't Be Afraid to Walk Away:

If the terms offered are not fair, remember you have the right to decline and seek better opportunities.

Navigating negotiations requires clarity, courage, and self-assurance. Understanding your worth and effectively communicating it can empower you to achieve the outcomes you deserve. Remember, your worth is non-negotiable—believe in yourself and go after your goals!

CONFRONTING BIAS AND DISCRIMINATION

Bias and discrimination in the workplace can feel isolating and overwhelming. However, confronting these challenges is both your right and within your power.

KEY REMINDERS:

- **You're Not Alone:** Many minority women face these challenges, and resources are available to support you.
- **You Are Worthy of Respect:** Your contributions matter, and you deserve to be treated with fairness and dignity.
- **You Have the Power to Create Change:** By advocating for yourself, you can inspire and pave the way for others.

PRACTICAL STRATEGIES

1. **Document Everything:** Keep detailed records of incidents, including dates, times, and specifics. Stay objective and focus on the facts.
2. **Speak Up:** If you feel comfortable, address the issue directly with the person involved. This can help resolve misunderstandings and prevent recurrence.

3. **Find Support:** Seek guidance from trusted colleagues, mentors, or HR representatives who can provide perspective and support.
4. **Know Your Rights:** Familiarize yourself with company policies and legal protections regarding discrimination and harassment.
5. **Don't Let It Define You:** Focus on your strengths, accomplishments, and goals rather than letting negative experiences dictate your self-worth.
6. **Practice Self-Care:** Prioritize activities that promote well-being and surround yourself with supportive individuals.
7. **Be an Advocate for Change:** Use your voice to promote inclusivity and participate in diversity initiatives.
8. **Find Your Voice:** Developing the confidence to speak up for yourself is essential. This doesn't mean being aggressive or confrontational, but it does require expressing your needs and boundaries with clarity and respect. This might include setting clear expectations, addressing microaggressions directly, or advocating for yourself during performance reviews and salary discussions.

9. **Don't Internalize the Bias:** Bias and discrimination can significantly impact your self-esteem, but it's vital to remember that the issue lies with the bias, not with you. You are talented, deserving, and worthy of respect. Don't allow others' opinions to diminish your sense of self-worth.

10. **Practice Assertiveness:** Assertiveness is a critical skill for addressing bias and discrimination. It empowers you to communicate your needs and boundaries confidently and respectfully without resorting to aggression or passivity. Being assertive can help you handle difficult conversations, set healthy boundaries, and effectively advocate for your needs.

11. **Utilize the Power of Storytelling:** Sharing your personal experiences with bias and discrimination can be a powerful way to inspire change. By educating others, raising awareness, and building empathy, your story can become a catalyst for action. Use your voice to share your journey and motivate others to stand against injustice.

EXAMPLES OF CONFRONTING BIAS AND DISCRIMINATION

Let's examine real-life scenarios that demonstrate effective ways to address bias and discrimination:

REAL-LIFE SCENARIOS

SCENARIO 1: "YOU'RE SO ARTICULATE!"

The Situation: You're in a meeting, presenting a project, and a colleague says, "Wow, you're so articulate!" While it may sound like a compliment, this statement can reinforce the stereotype that minority women are valued only for their verbal skills rather than their intelligence or competence.

THE RESPONSE:

- Acknowledge the comment but address the underlying assumption:

"Thank you! I'm passionate about this project, and I'm glad my communication skills are helpful."

Shift the focus to your broader contributions:

"I've also been working hard on the data analysis and research, and I'm happy to share those insights with the team."

- Use humor (if appropriate):

"I'm not surprised you're impressed. My articulation skills are top-notch!"

SCENARIO 2: THE "TOKEN" MINORITY

The Situation: You're the only person of color in your department and are frequently asked to represent your culture or speak on behalf of all minority employees. This is an example of tokenism, where individuals from underrepresented groups are used as symbols of inclusivity but are not genuinely integrated into the company culture.

THE RESPONSE:

- Set clear boundaries:

"While I'm happy to share my perspective, I'm not comfortable being the sole representative of all minority employees. My skills and expertise go beyond my cultural background."

- Redirect the conversation toward broader diversity and inclusion efforts:

"It's important to have diverse perspectives and experiences at the table. Let's discuss ways to create a more inclusive environment for everyone."

SCENARIO 3: MICROAGGRESSIONS IN A PERFORMANCE REVIEW

The Situation: During a performance review, your manager emphasizes your "soft skills" and interpersonal abilities but overlooks your technical contributions to the project. This subtle bias can downplay your technical expertise and reinforce gender stereotypes.

THE RESPONSE:

- **Address the Bias:** Acknowledge the praise but redirect attention to your technical achievements: "I appreciate your feedback on my communication skills, but I'd also like to discuss my contributions to the technical aspects of the project."

- **Provide Specific Examples:** Highlight your accomplishments with concrete details: "For instance, I led the development of [specific project component], which resulted in [positive outcome]."

- **Request Technical Feedback:** Open the door for constructive input on your technical abilities: "Could you share feedback on my performance in areas like [specific technical skill or responsibility]?"

NAVIGATING THE EMOTIONAL TOLL

Confronting bias and discrimination can be emotionally taxing, making it essential to care for your mental and emotional well-being during this process.

- **Seek Professional Support:** Consider connecting with a therapist or counselor. They can help you process emotions, develop coping strategies, and gain clarity on your experiences.
- **Build a Supportive Network:** Surround yourself with other minority women or like-minded peers who can offer empathy, encouragement, and a sense of community.
- **Practice Self-Care:** Prioritize activities that bring you peace and relaxation. Whether it's yoga, meditation, spending time in nature, or engaging in hobbies, focus on nurturing your emotional health.

BUILDING A MORE INCLUSIVE WORKPLACE

Beyond addressing individual instances of bias, you can take steps to foster a more inclusive work environment.

- **Advocate for Diversity Initiatives:** Share ideas in meetings, participate in company-sponsored events, and support efforts aimed at creating equity in the workplace.

- **Promote Mentorship:** Offer mentorship to other minority women or connect with senior leaders who can mentor and guide emerging talent.
- **Support External Organizations:** Contribute time, resources, or advocacy to organizations dedicated to promoting diversity and inclusion.

FINDING YOUR VOICE

As you navigate the complexities of confronting bias and discrimination, remember that your voice is a powerful tool for change.

- **Draw Strength from Resilience:** Your intelligence, determination, and unique experiences are your strengths. Use them to advocate for yourself and others.
- **Inspire Action:** Speak up, share your story, and encourage others to join in creating a fairer and more equitable workplace.
- **Lean on Resources:** Remember that you are not alone in this journey. Allies, communities, and support systems are there to assist you every step of the way.

Embrace your strengths, stand firm, and know that you can drive meaningful change.

PROMOTING INCLUSIVITY AND DIVERSITY

The push for an inclusive and diverse workplace isn't just a passing trend; it's a necessary shift for real progress. You've already explored how to identify and address biases and microaggressions, and now it's time to take an active role in fostering a fair and equitable environment—not just for yourself, but because it's the right thing to do.

Imagine a workplace where diversity isn't tokenistic but a dynamic exchange of experiences and perspectives. A space where every voice is heard, every talent is valued, and everyone feels empowered to contribute meaningfully. This vision is achievable, one deliberate action at a time.

HOW TO BECOME A CHAMPION FOR INCLUSIVITY

1. Speak Up: Your Voice Matters

Remaining silent in the face of injustice perpetuates the status quo. Speaking up can challenge biases, inspire conversations, and drive change.

- **Call Out Microaggressions:** Use clear, non-confrontational language to address inappropriate behavior. For example, "I felt uncomfortable with that comment because it perpetuates harmful stereotypes about my community."

- **Challenge Exclusionary Language:** Pay attention to the words used in meetings or communications. If something feels exclusive or biased, suggest more inclusive alternatives.
- **Offer Support and Allyship:** Stand with colleagues who have faced discrimination or harassment by listening without judgment and offering encouragement.

2. Champion Diversity in Hiring and Promotions

Inclusivity isn't just about representation; it's about creating equitable opportunities for growth and advancement.

- **Address Bias in Recruitment:** Advocate for inclusive job descriptions, diverse candidate pools, and unbiased interview processes.
- **Speak Out Against Tokenism:** Tokenism involves including a small number of individuals from underrepresented groups to give the illusion of diversity without making meaningful strides toward equality. When you encounter tokenism, address it directly and advocate for true inclusion that values diverse perspectives and ensures equity.
- **Champion Equitable Promotion Practices:** Ensure that promotion decisions based on merit

and performance, free from the influence of race, gender, or other irrelevant factors.

3. Build an Inclusive Culture

Creating a genuinely inclusive culture is an ongoing effort requiring open communication, education, and accountability.

- **Celebrate Diversity:** Host events and initiatives that highlight the unique backgrounds, experiences, and perspectives of your team.
- **Encourage Empathy and Understanding:** Support programs like cultural exchanges, mentorship initiatives, or diversity training to broaden perspectives and build stronger connections.
- **Listen to Marginalized Voices:** Actively seek input from underrepresented groups and use their feedback to improve company policies and practices.

4. Be a Role Model

As a woman of color, your journey can inspire others and demonstrate the impact of authentic, inclusive leadership.

- **Embrace Authenticity:** Lead confidently, staying true to your experiences, perspectives, and strengths.
- **Mentor and Support Others:** Help colleagues facing similar challenges by sharing your insights and creating a safe space for growth.
- **Advocate for Equity:** Speak out against biases and push for systemic change that benefits everyone.

BEYOND THE WORKPLACE

Your commitment to inclusivity doesn't have to stop at the office. There are many ways to make an impact in your community:

- **Volunteer with Advocacy Organizations:** Offer your time and skills to groups that empower underrepresented communities.
- **Mentor Young Women of Color:** Share your experiences and guidance with the next generation of leaders.
- **Raise Awareness:** Use your voice and platform to spotlight issues affecting marginalized groups and push for actionable change.

Remember, your voice matters. Your actions can drive meaningful change toward a more inclusive and equitable world. By standing up, speaking out, and championing diversity, you contribute to creating a workplace where everyone has the opportunity to thrive and give their best. This isn't solely about your own success—it's about building success for all.

THE PATH FORWARD

The journey toward an inclusive and equitable workplace is ongoing. It requires awareness, consistent effort, and a willingness to learn. Remember, you're not alone—many others share your vision of a more just world.

Build alliances, connect with like-minded individuals, and support organizations committed to inclusivity. Together, we can create workplaces that celebrate diversity, normalize inclusion, and empower everyone to achieve their goals.

CELEBRATING SUCCESS AND GROWTH

The path to growth and success is rarely a straight line. It's a winding road filled with twists, turns, and moments of doubt. But within these challenges lie opportunities to build resilience, sharpen your skills, and emerge stronger than ever. This chapter is about celebrating the victories—big and small—that have shaped your journey. It's a moment to acknowledge your progress, honor your efforts, and embrace the empowering experiences that have brought you to where you are today.

Think back to the day you landed your first job—the excitement, the nervous anticipation, and the thrill of starting a new chapter in your professional life. That moment of accomplishment became the foundation upon which you built your career. Along the way, you faced obstacles, learned from mistakes, and adapted to the ever-evolving demands of your industry.

Each challenge you tackled, each lesson you learned, and every hurdle you overcame became stepping stones on your path to success.

RECOGNIZING YOUR PROGRESS

Take a moment to reflect on the skills you've acquired. Perhaps you improved your communication, mastered new software, or deepened your knowledge in your field. Maybe you initiated a project, championed an important cause, or stood up for inclusivity in your workplace. These achievements, no matter the size, contribute to your personal and professional growth.

Think of a time you faced a difficult client or tackled a challenging project. You might have felt overwhelmed, doubted your abilities, or considered giving up. But you didn't. You relied on your resourcefulness, drew from your experience, and found a way through. These moments, no matter how tough, helped shape your character and strengthened your resolve.

Celebrate the times you stepped outside your comfort zone—whether by taking on a leadership role, presenting to a large audience, or voicing your opinion in a meeting. Though intimidating at first, these experiences helped you grow, expand your horizons, and uncover hidden strengths.

THE IMPORTANCE OF GRATITUDE

As you reflect on your journey, take a moment to recognize the people who supported you. Friends, family, mentors, and allies have been there to offer encouragement, guidance, and a listening ear. Their belief in you has played a significant role in your success. Remember to express gratitude for their contributions—it strengthens your relationships and honors their support.

Celebrating your successes isn't about bragging. It's about acknowledging your hard work, appreciating your resilience, and recognizing the unique path that has brought you here. It's about

celebrating the person you've become—strong, capable, and ready to achieve even more.

FROM SMALL WINS TO MAJOR MILESTONES

Every step forward contributes to the bigger picture of your success. Even small victories—a well-executed project, a successful presentation, or learning a new skill—are essential building blocks.

- **Appreciating Small Wins:** Think back to when you grasped a complex concept or learned a new tool. These moments boosted your confidence and encouraged you to keep pushing forward.
- **Acknowledging Achievements:** Take time to celebrate your progress. A small reward, a moment of reflection, or simply acknowledging your effort can reinvigorate your motivation.
- **Sharing Successes:** Share your wins with others to spread positivity and inspire those around you. It not only amplifies your joy but also encourages others to pursue and celebrate their achievements.

BUILDING A CULTURE OF EMPOWERMENT

Celebrating your success isn't just a personal endeavor; it's also about fostering a culture of empowerment within your workplace and community.

- **Support Your Colleagues:** Encourage underrepresented or marginalized colleagues to celebrate their achievements. Acknowledge their contributions and create an environment where sharing successes feels safe and welcomed.
- **Mentor and Sponsor:** Share your knowledge and experience by mentoring others. Help them navigate challenges and reach their own goals.
- **Advocate for Equity:** Promote a workplace culture that values diversity and inclusion. Celebrate the successes of individuals from different backgrounds and ensure everyone feels appreciated and empowered.

EMBRACING GROWTH

Celebrating success is not only about reflecting on past achievements with pride; it's also about looking ahead with purpose and excitement. It means adopting a mindset focused on progress, recognizing that success is not a fixed destination but an ongoing journey of learning, adaptation, and striving for new goals.

CONTINUOUS LEARNING

Commit to lifelong learning by actively seeking opportunities to enhance your knowledge, skills, and perspectives. Growth is an ongoing process, and there is always room for improvement and development in every stage of life.

- **Commit to Lifelong Learning:** Keep expanding your knowledge and skills. There's always room for growth and new opportunities to explore.
- **Stay Curious:** Be open to new ideas, technologies, and approaches. Curiosity keeps you innovative and adaptable.
- **Set New Goals:** Celebrate your achievements, but don't stop there. Challenge yourself to reach higher and strive for continual improvement.

THE POWER OF CELEBRATING SUCCESS

Recognizing your achievements is a crucial part of your personal and professional journey. It helps you appreciate your progress, maintain a positive mindset, and build the confidence to aim for even greater heights. Success isn't just about the destination—it's about the journey, the lessons learned, and the victories celebrated along the way.

ACKNOWLEDGMENTS

This book would not have been possible without the countless individuals who inspired, supported, and challenged me along the way. To the remarkable minority women who shared their stories, vulnerabilities, and triumphs—you are the soul of this work. Your courage and resilience serve as a beacon of hope and empowerment for us all.

My heartfelt gratitude goes to my mentors, friends, and family, whose steadfast encouragement and belief in my vision have been invaluable. Thank you for your insightful feedback, unwavering support, and the love that fuels my passion.

A special thanks to the editors and publishing team at The Champagne Connection for your expertise, guidance, and dedication to bringing this book to fruition. Your commitment and professionalism made this journey seamless and fulfilling.

Finally, I dedicate this book to all minority women striving for success and leaving their mark on the world. May this work serve as a source of inspiration, a guide to achieving your goals, and a testament to the strength and brilliance within you.

APPENDIX

This appendix provides additional resources and tools for continued learning and support. It includes:

LIST OF SEVERAL ORGANIZATIONS SUPPORTING MINORITY WOMEN

This list contains contact information for national and local organizations dedicated to empowering minority women in business, education, and community development.

NATIONAL COALITION OF 100 BLACK WOMEN (NCBW)

Focus: Advocates on behalf of Black women and girls to promote leadership development and gender equity in areas of health, education, and economic empowerment.

Website: ncbw.org

ASSOCIATION OF LATINO PROFESSIONALS FOR AMERICA (ALPFA)

Focus: Provides professional development and networking for Latina women.

Website: alpfa.org

NATIONAL ASIAN PACIFIC AMERICAN WOMEN'S FORUM (NAPAWF)

Focus: Advocates for social justice and equity for Asian Pacific American women and girls.

Website: napawf.org

BLACK GIRLS CODE

Focus: Provides African American girls with opportunities to learn programming and technology skills.

Website: blackgirlscode.com

YWCA USA

Focus: Eliminates racism, empowers women, and promotes peace, justice, freedom, and dignity.

Website: ywca.org

RECOMMENDED READING

Below is a partial list of books, articles, and websites that offer further insights on topics covered in this book.

PERSONAL DEVELOPMENT & SELF-EMPOWERMENT

1. **"Becoming" by Michelle Obama**

   A memoir from the former First Lady that provides inspiration and insight into overcoming challenges and pursuing excellence.

2. **"You Are Your Best Thing" edited by Tarana Burke and Brené Brown**

   A collection of essays on vulnerability, resilience, and self-care, particularly for women of color.

3. **"The Year of Yes" by Shonda Rhimes**

   Chronicles how saying "yes" to opportunities transformed the life of this celebrated television producer.

4. **"More Than Enough" by Elaine Welteroth**

   Shares lessons in owning one's identity and thriving as a woman of color in white-dominated spaces.

LEADERSHIP & CAREER ADVANCEMENT

5. **"Lead from the Outside" by Stacey Abrams**

   A practical guide for minorities, women, and others traditionally excluded from power to make an impact.

6. **"Own It: The Power of Women at Work" by Sallie Krawcheck**

   Advice for women on succeeding in the workplace, particularly in male-dominated fields.

7. **"Lean In: Women, Work, and the Will to Lead" by Sheryl Sandberg**

   Insights and advice for women navigating the workplace, with added relevance for minority women working through intersectional challenges.

8. **"Dare to Lead" by Brené Brown**

   Encourages cultivating courage and empathy as tools for transformative leadership.

ENTREPRENEURSHIP & FINANCIAL SUCCESS

9. **"The Memo: What Women of Color Need to Know to Secure a Seat at the Table" by Minda Harts**

   A practical career guide tailored to the experiences of women of color.

10. **"We Should All Be Millionaires" by Rachel Rodgers**

    A roadmap for women, especially women of color, to build wealth and financial independence.

11. **"Side Hustle Pro" by Nicaila Matthews Okome**
    o Insights into starting and growing successful side hustles, from one of the leading voices on the topic.

RESILIENCE & MENTAL WELLNESS

12. **"Radical Self-Love" by Sonya Renee Taylor**

    Promotes embracing one's identity and body as part of the path to empowerment.

13. **"Set Boundaries, Find Peace" by Nedra Glover Tawwab**

    A guide to asserting boundaries, essential for mental health and professional success.

14. **"Unapologetically Ambitious" by Shellye Archambeau**

    A story of resilience and determination from one of Silicon Valley's first Black female CEOs.

INSPIRATIONAL STORIES

15. **"I Am Malala" by Malala Yousafzai**

    Chronicles the journey of a young girl advocating for education and empowerment in the face of adversity.

16. **"Hood Feminism: Notes from the Women That a Movement Forgot" by Mikki Kendall**

    A critique of mainstream feminism with a focus on issues affecting women of color.

17. **"The Beauty of Breaking" by Michele Harper**

    A memoir by a Black ER physician, touching on resilience, healing, and finding one's path.

FINANCIAL LITERACY RESOURCES

Links to online resources, workshops, and financial advisors specializing in financial literacy for women.

ORGANIZATIONS AND PROGRAMS

1. **Operation HOPE**

    Focus: Financial literacy and empowerment for underserved communities, including minority women.

    Programs: Credit counseling, financial coaching, small business workshops.

    Website: operationhope.org

2. **Savvy Ladies**

    Focus: Provides free financial education and support to women.

Resources: Free financial helpline, webinars, workshops, and one-on-one financial planning.

Website: savvyladies.org

3. My Money My Future (MMMF)

Focus: Financial planning resources for women of color, with tools for managing credit, budgeting, and investments.

Programs: Online courses, blogs, and financial planning tools.

Website: mymoneymyfuture.co

4. Black Women's Wealth Alliance (BWWA)

Focus: Supports Black women in building wealth through financial literacy and entrepreneurship.

Programs: Financial wellness workshops, small business grants, and investment guidance.

Website: blackwomenswealthalliance.org

5. Women's Institute for Financial Education (WIFE)

Focus: Financial education specifically tailored for women.

Resources: Articles, tools, and workshops on budgeting, retirement, and investment.

Website: wife.org

WORKSHOPS AND COACHING

6. **Girlboss Financial Workshops**

   Focus: Offers financial literacy courses for women, emphasizing empowerment and actionable strategies.

   Website: girlboss.com

7. **Her Money**

   Focus: Provides practical financial advice for women, including podcasts, workshops, and resources.

   Website: hermoney.com

8. **She's on the Money**

   Focus: Financial empowerment for women with a focus on building wealth and financial independence.

   Website: shesonthemoney.com.au

ADVISORS AND NETWORKS

9. **Certified Financial Planners (CFP®)**

   Focus: Use the CFP® Finder Tool to locate minority or women advisors near you. Many specialize in diverse communities and women's financial needs.

10. **Ellevest**

    Founder: Sallie Krawcheck

Focus: A digital investment platform designed for women, offering coaching and financial planning services.

Website: ellevest.com

11. **Latina Money**

Focus: Financial literacy programs and tools for Latina women to build wealth and financial security.

Website: latinamoney.com

BOOKS AND ONLINE COURSES

12. **"We Should All Be Millionaires" by Rachel Rodgers**

A guide to wealth-building for women, especially women of color.

Website: helloseven.co

13. **YNAB (You Need A Budget)**

Offers budgeting tools and courses that cater to beginners and advanced financial planners alike.

Website: ynab.com

14. **Black Women Invest**

   A community promoting investment education and financial growth for Black women.

   Website: blackwomeninvest.org

COMMUNITY AND SOCIAL MEDIA

15. **Instagram and TikTok Financial Educators**

Follow creators like:

- @TheBudgetnista (Tiffany Aliche): Financial literacy for women.
- @CleverGirlFinance: Financial advice and empowerment for women of color.

GLOSSARY

Microaggression: Subtle, often unintentional actions or behaviors that convey prejudice or discrimination toward members of marginalized groups.

Tokenism: The practice of making superficial or symbolic efforts to include members of minority groups without providing meaningful inclusion or equality.

Implicit Bias: Unconscious prejudices or stereotypes that influence attitudes and behaviors, often operating without our conscious awareness.

Intersectionality: The interconnected nature of social categorizations—such as race, gender, class, and sexual orientation—that create overlapping and interdependent systems of discrimination or disadvantage.

Allyship: The active and intentional support of marginalized groups by individuals outside those groups, working to dismantle systemic barriers and promote equity and inclusion.

ABOUT THE AUTHOR ...

STEPHANIE WILSON-COLEMAN, D.D., PH.D.

With an Executive MBA from the University of Chicago Booth School of Business, a Ph.D. in Holistic Life Counseling, and certifications, including Behavioral Finance from Duke University, Dr. Stephanie brings over two decades of proven leadership experience. As a former National Director for a Federal Agency, she played a pivotal role in enhancing employee performance, shaping strategic visions, and driving high-impact results. She also served on the Presidential Transition Teams in 2013 and 2017 and is a proud member of Alpha Kappa Alpha Sorority, Incorporated.

Today, Dr. Stephanie thrives as a Speaker and Corporate Trainer, empowering organizations to cultivate emerging leaders. She utilizes her OCEAN and Boat Framework to help organizations develop succession strategies with her signature program, "Navigating Tomorrow: Steering Your Succession Strategy to Calmer Waters."

Dr. Stephanie's expertise has been recognized by major media outlets, including ABC, NBC, CBS, WGN, UpJourney Magazine, and Authority Magazine. She is also a prolific author, having written five books. Her latest work, "Self-Esteem Your Superpower: Ways Parents Can Improve Children's Self-Esteem," achieved #1 Amazon best-seller status in four categories for four consecutive weeks.

Resilience defines Dr. Stephanie's journey. She has triumphed over profound adversities, including sexual molestation, becoming a mother at 14, experiencing homelessness, surviving a traumatic brain injury, and enduring the tragic loss of her son.

Dr. Stephanie inspires others with her powerful message:

"Adversity may write the first chapters of our story, but resilience pens the triumphant ending, turning every setback into a stepping stone. on the path to *success."*

www.ingramcontent.com/pod-product-compliance
Lightning Source LLC
Chambersburg PA
CBHW072044160426
43197CB00014B/2621